Architecture + Advocacy

Architecture + Advocacy

Robert Traynham Coles, FAIA

Photo: David Gordon

Compiled and Edited by
William H. Siener, PhD
with Sylvia Coles

Buffalo Arts Publishing

 Buffalo Arts Publishing

Architecture + Advocacy, Robert Traynham Coles, FAIA. Copyright © 2016 by Robert Traynham Coles. All rights reserved. Printed in the United States of America. No part of this book may be used or reproduced in any manner whatsoever without written permission. For information, address Buffalo Arts Publishing, 179 Greenfield Drive, Tonawanda, NY 14150.

Email: info@buffaloartspublishing.com

Cover design based on a photograph by Sylvia Coles of the skylight in the lobby of the Frank E. Merriweather, Jr., branch library, Buffalo, NY.

Publisher's Cataloging-in-Publication data

Names: Coles, Robert Traynham, author. | Siener, William H., editor. | Coles, Sylvia, editor.

Title: Architecture and advocacy / Robert Traynham Coles, FAIA ; compiled and edited by William H. Siener, PhD ; with Sylvia Coles.

Description: Includes index. | Tonawanda, NY: Buffalo Arts Publishing, 2016.

Identifiers: ISBN 978-0997874105 | LCCN 2016946261

Subjects: LCSH Coles, Robert Traynham. | Architects--United States--Biography. | African American architects. | Architecture and race--United States. | Space (Architecture)--Social aspects--United States. | BISAC ARCHITECTURE / Individual Architects & Firms / General | BIOGRAPHY & AUTOBIOGRAPHY / Artists, Architects, Photographers.

Classification: LCC NA738.N5 .C65 2016 | DDC 720.89/96073--dc23

10 9 8 7 6 5 4 3 2 1

Dedicated to the memory of Dr. Jesse Edward Nash, Jr.

CONTENTS

List of Illustrations .... page ix

Editor's Foreword xi

The Circle and the Square by Richard Dozier xiii

Introduction 1

Chapter 1: Influences and Opportunities 3

Chapter 2: The Firm: Founding and Philosophy 13

Chapter 3: An Activist Matures 21

Chapter 4: The Firm: New Challenges, New Directions 29

Chapter 5: Educator, Advocate, Services to the Profession 37

Chapter 6: Recognition and Unfinished Business 49

Appendix A – Honors & Awards 55

Appendix B – Project Listing 59

Appendix C – Selected Projects 63

Appendix D – African American Architects/Interns 85

Appendix E – Published Articles 89

    An Architect Looks at Buffalo by Robert Traynham Coles 91
    First published in *Buffalo Business*, October, 1963

    The Impact of an Architect by Linda Levine 97
    First published in *Buffalo Spree*, 1981

    Black Architects, An Endangered Species by Robert Traynham Coles ... 101
    First published in *Progressive Architecture Magazine*, July, 1989

    Urban Waterfront and Public Access by Robert Traynham Coles 103
    An address for the *Sam Gibbons Eminent Scholar's Chair Lectures
    in Architecture and Urban Planning*, February, 1990

    My Experience as an African American Architect, and Prospects for the Future 107
    A talk by Robert T. Coles at Howard University, February, 2001

    Buffalo By Architecture by Kelly Hayes McAlonie 113
    First published in *Buffalo Spree Home*, July, 2011

Acknowledgments 117

Index 119

Special Thanks 124

Illustrations

Robert Traynham Coles .... Title Page
Design Diaspora logo, designed by Carolyn Armenta Davis .... page xii
Robert Traynham Coles, PC logo xii
Robert Traynham Coles at his desk 1
RTC behind model of JFK Recreation Center 2
Richfield State Bank 4
Rapson, Coles, Fisher 5
Rotch Scholarship trip: RTC and SC w/Darcy 6
Rotch Scholarship trip: Coles station wagon in Italy 6
Winning design for Rotch Scholarship 7
Sterling Forest Techbuilt home 8
Coles home, front 9
Coles home, rear 11
Coles home, upper floor plan 11
Coles home, lower floor plan 11
JFK Recreation Center 12
Multi-purpose room of JFK Recreation Center 12
Joseph J. Kelly Gardens housing complex 14
Solomon Court, Buffalo, NY 14
Sample Memorial Playground, Chautauqua, NY 15
Berlyn residence in Worcester, Mass 16
Wright/Evans weekend house in Attica, NY 16
Eppolito Residence in Orchard Park, NY 17
R. Buckminster Fuller's plan for SUNY at Buffalo phys ed complex 17
1970s staff photo 19
Richard Prosser and Robert Coles 20
Friendship House 21
Juneteenth Festival 22
ESCO leadership team - Coles, Wright, Alinsky, Ford 23
Whitney M. Young, Jr. 24
Coles with Cleon Service, Janet and Richard Prosser at CPAC headquarters, Buffalo, NY ... 25
William Thaddeus Coleman 27
SUNY at Buffalo Alumni Arena (2 photos) 28
Black American Museum and Cultural Center, Niagara Falls 29
Lindbergh Center MARTA Station 30
Frank Reeves Center (3 photos) 31
Utica Street Subway Station 32
Health, Phys. Ed, and Recreation, Alumni Arena at SUNYAB 33
Alumni Arena Natatorium 33
William Emslie YMCA 34
William Emslie YMCA, upper level plan 34
William Emslie YMCA, lower level plan 34
Bidwell Station Post Office 35
Gowanda Psychiatric Center Rehab Treatment Center 35

Illustrations cont'd

Robert Coles with Lenore Bethel at BECHS Museum	36
Dr. Wilbert Le Melle with Sylvia and Robert Coles	38
Roberta Washington and Norma Sklarek	39
RTC becomes Chancellor of College of Fellows	40
Coles, Vosbeck, and Prigmore at RTC's Chancellorship celebration	41
Johnnie B. Wiley Pavilion, Buffalo, NY	42
Public School 233, Brooklyn, NY	42
Ronald H. Brown Pavilion, Harlem, NY	43
Amistad comes to Buffalo (3 photos)	44
Jesse Nash, Diana Dillaway, Robert Coles	44
The Tile Quilt, Apollo Theater Project, Buffalo, NY	45
Frank E. Merriweather, Jr., Branch Library	45
Proposed Kigutu Health Center, Bujumbura, Burundi	46
Merriweather Library floor plan	47
Kigutu Clinic floor plan	47
Medals awarded to Robert Coles	48
Peter Fleischmann, Robert Coles, Richard Dozier, David Gordon	50
Robert Traynham Coles section of Brent Exhibition, BPAC	50
Plaque Dedication for Louise Bethune	51
Dr. Sharon Sutton at the 2011 AIA Convention in New Orleans	52
Paul Devrouax, Marshall Purnell, R. Randall Vosbeck, Robert Coles	53
Coles receiving Whitney Young Citation from R. Randall Vosbeck	55
Whitney M. Young, Jr. Citation	58
JFK Recreation Center	64
Townsend Dental Clinic	65
Friendship House	66
Joseph J. Kelly Gardens Housing for the Elderly	67
Paul Lindsay Sample Memorial Playground, Chautauqua Institute	68
Urban Park Housing Development, Rochester, NY	69
New Elementary School No. 40	70
William-Emslie YMCA, Buffalo, NY	71
Operations Control Center and South Park Yards & Shops, NFTA, Buffalo, NY	72
Lindbergh Center Station, Atlanta, GA	73
Health, Physical Education & Recreation Complex, Phase I, Alumni Arena	74
Health, Physical Education & Recreation Complex, Phase II, Natatorium	75
Providence Station, Providence, RI	76-77
Frank Reeves Center for Municipal Affairs, Washington, D.C.	78
Asarese-Matters Community Center	79
Rehab Treatment Center, Gowanda Psychiatric Center	80
Human Services Office Building, Canandaigua, NY	81
Ronald H. Brown Pavilion, Harlem, NY	82
City of Buffalo Telecommunications Center	83
Frank E. Merriweather, Jr. Branch Library, Buffalo, NY	84
Robert Coles and Lewis Harriman, "Happiness is a Waterfront University"	105
NYS Assemblyman Arthur O. Eve with Robert Coles	116

Editor's Foreword

OUR mutual friend, Jesse Nash, introduced me to Bob Coles about 20 years ago. Bob graciously provided some pictures of his home, and some insights about its design for an exhibit that I was working on at the time. However, it was not for another ten years or so that our friendship really blossomed. Bob and I both were deeply involved with the planning of a 2003 visit by the Freedom Schooner *Amistad* to Buffalo. I found his enthusiasm for the project infectious, and it buoyed me up at times when I thought that some of the obstacles to its success were insurmountable.

Bob's extroverted enthusiasm for tackling problems and issues head-on, the opposite of my own cautious approach, was what drew me to him. Topics over lunch ranged from his reminiscences about working on the railroad to earn money for college, to publishing a revised edition of the *Buffalo Architecture Guidebook*, to memories of his childhood, including swimming at the Michigan Avenue YMCA. We also collaborated on a couple of proposals for some architectural projects that would have needed historical research. Sadly, those did not come to fruition. It would have been fun to have worked with him in that capacity. I even was drawn in, in a very minor way, to reviewing with him some of his strategies for attracting more minorities to architecture. I was not much help, but sometimes a good listener is useful.

Over the course of several summers, we also enjoyed many afternoons of sailing on Bob's beloved *Moorjoy*, the boat that led the flotilla that welcomed *Amistad* to Buffalo.

Bob has always enjoyed writing, and was good at it. When he traveled to conferences, on business trips, and for pleasure, he often wrote a one- or two-page reflection about highlights of the trip, and what the trip had meant to him. It is a discipline I wish I could implement. His essays like *An Architect Looks at Buffalo, and Black Architects: An Endangered Species*, show him to be thoughtful, insightful, and precise—not to mention witty. Were it not for advancing age, he would have compiled and written this book on his own. It is written in the third person, but it is HIS memoir. I have done my best to play the role of amanuensis rather than historian or biographer. I have reviewed original source material from his personal records and from his firm, and the things Bob has written about architecture in general, and about being an African American architect. I have also read much that journalists, friends, and colleagues have written about him. Most of all, to the best of my ability, I have listened to Bob tell me about his experience and career. I hope that the text tells his story the way he wants it told, and the way he would have told it himself.

William H. Siener, Ph.D.
Buffalo, NY, January 2016

Robert Traynham Coles, Architect, PC was selected to be one of fifty prominent Black architectural firms from eleven countries included in *Design Diaspora: Black Architects and International Architecture (1970-1990)*, a traveling exhibition, curated by Carolyn Armenta Davis and organized by The Chicago Athenaeum, an international museum of architecture and design, with support from the Lila Wallace Reader's Digest Fund. The historic exhibition debuted in 1993 in Chicago and toured to 20 venues on 4 continents. The 18 May - 14 July 1996, Buffalo, NY, presentation was hosted by the Burchfield Penney Art Center, and was an important venue for the global tour.

The Circle and the Square:
Robert Traynham Coles, FAIA

by Dr. Richard K. Dozier, AIA

The poetry of Langston Hughes often addresses the history and tradition of African-American builders and architects.

> *I've known rivers:*
> *I've known rivers ancient as the world and older than the flow of human blood in human veins.*
> *My soul has grown deep like the rivers...*
> *I build my hut near the Congo...*
> *I looked upon the Nile and raised the pyramids above it.*
>   Langston Hughes, "The Negro Speaks of Rivers," 1925.
>
> *Under my hands the pyramids rose...*
> *I made the mortar for the Woolworth building...*
>   Langston Hughes, "I am a Negro, " 1925.

Robert Traynham Coles' office logo utilizes nine pronounced black squares on a white background with the seventh square slightly skewed. The firm's logo immediately engages the viewer and forces a struggle to define its many implications. Does it imply marching to a different drummer? The "seventh son"? Does it suggest a new or different approach? Or is it but another variation of the "skewed grid, " so often implied and utilized by contemporary architects? We are immediately struck by the considerable implications of this skillful and subtle design. Equally engaging are the implications of consistency and continuity implied with the circle form in the Design Diaspora exhibit logo. Combined, the logos prepare the visitor for the dynamic range of international, national, and local accomplishments of work by architects of African descent. That the need for these exhibitions is long overdue is indicated by historian Michael Adams, who stated: "Despite over 200 years of involvement in the building of America, the historical contributions of Black designers remains obscure."[1]

The use of such strong geometry in the logos is more than coincidence. The circle of Design Diaspora implies the long tradition and continuity of architects of African descent, which expresses the exhibit's intention to be "a tribute to the achievements of the thousands of unheralded Black architects – male and female; past, present, and future – who have created and continue to create contextual, solution-oriented architecture that enriches the human spirit and environment."

Robert Traynham Coles has described African-American architects as an "endangered species." A local and national trailblazer, Coles has built his way to the top of the profession.[2] When Coles began his practice in 1963, some 233 African-American architects operated less than 50 architectural firms in the country. Since that time, Coles has emerged as an educator, mentor, and leader in his field. He was elected to the American Institute of Architects (AIA) College of Fellows in 1981, and in 1995 he was elected Chancellor of that prestigious organization, the first African-American to be so honored.

The exhibited projects reflect the history, progress, and consistent urban commitment of Coles' firm. They also provide a brief, but significant view of the struggle of African-American architects. Equally important, with images of brick and mortar the exhibit heightens our curiosity for a broader understanding of the African-American architect in the Queen City of the Lakes. What has been the contribution of the African-American architect in this city famed for architectural statements of Frank Lloyd Wright, Louis Sullivan, H. H. Richardson, and Louise Blanchard Bethune, the nation's first female architect?

A product of ethnic industrial Buffalo, Coles knew little of these architects when he embarked on architectural studies. As a student at Buffalo's premier Technical High School, he was sidetracked into building design. After high school, Coles departed for Hampton Institute, the Virginia school attended by Booker T. Washington, followed by the University of Minnesota to continue his architectural studies. By the time he returned to Buffalo in 1963, Coles had completed one year of study and travel in Europe, as well as his masters degree in architecture at the Massachusetts Institute of Technology.

Coles' designs for the John F. Kennedy Recreation Center and his own residence mark the beginning of the architect's Buffalo practice of thirty-plus years. This exhibit focuses on three major periods in Coles' career. Varying both in scale and location, the projects reflect Coles' strong commitment to public service and community involvement. The large number of public and governmental projects in both exhibits suggest a paradox of the Black architect: an opportunity to impact on his/her community, but much too often being limited or excluded from major private commissions and fees.

Bob Coles' return to Buffalo marked a milestone in the beginning of the rebuilding of Buffalo 's urban core. His MIT thesis in part had focused on urban renewal and the design of recreational facilities. The study centered on Buffalo's Ellicott Renewal district. Coles' very first projects during these early years are centered around this early Black community and its history. Five years after the historic Niagara Movement meeting in 1905, the established Black community in Buffalo – almost invisible throughout the 19th century – had expanded to 1,773. The 1920 census reported 59 Black architects in the country. In 1930, the number increased to 63. By the late 1920s, 2 of those 63 Black architects had relocated to Buffalo. William L. Evans (1885-1966)[3] and John E. Brent (1889-1962) were among the varied professionals and laborers who had swelled the Queen City's Black population beyond 9,000.

The names of early Coles' projects conjure up images of members of the Buffalo Pantheon of African-American heroes and heroines – names such as Geneva B. Scruggs, Sherman L. Walker, and Reverend Jesse E. Nash. Each of these individuals played a pivotal role in the development of Buffalo's historic Eastside African American community. As far back as 1830, the tight area between Broadway and William Street on Michigan Avenue became the center. By the 20th century, Montgomery's Little Harlem, Michigan Avenue Baptist Church, Roger Smith's Drugs, and the Club Moonglow were among its landmark structures. During the years preceding the depression, Blacks moved west along Michigan Avenue. During this period the famed Michigan YMCA, designed by pioneering Buffalo African-American architect John Brent, was constructed. Unfortunately, this move west and the impact of the depression further contributed to the area's decline. In 1975 the Michigan Avenue YMCA was demolished. With the recent loss of Montgomery's Little Harlem, only the tiny red brick Michigan Avenue Baptist Church remains of these historic structures.

Fortunately, in 1982 Robert Coles received the commission for the William-Emslie YMCA, which was intended in part to replace the historic Michigan Avenue building. Coles' design for the Williams-Emslie continues the tradition of the Michigan Avenue YMCA by providing a multipurpose facility for that community.

Over the past fifteen years Coles has expanded his horizons to include architectural offices in Washington, D.C., and New York City. A significant collaboration involving a majority firm and the Black architectural firm of Devrouax and Purnell Architects resulted in the $35,000,000 Frank Reeves Center for Municipal Affairs in Washington's urban area. It was heralded as a bold and innovative solution. In addition, Coles, a sought-after lecturer, commutes regularly to architecture schools in Kansas, Pennsylvania, and Florida.

Coles often speaks of a broad approach to architecture. He once said he saw himself not as a Black architect, but as an architect who was Black. He would later restate it to say he saw himself as "a Black architect." We all have benefited from Coles' vision and leadership in the profession and in our cities. In his work and philosophy Robert Traynham Coles links us to those whose record of struggle on the playing field of architecture in Western New York has been all but annihilated. Although Coles, as the Langston Hughes scholar, has spoken of the Black architect as an endangered species, he, like Langston Hughes, has preserved and made a living at his art.[4] Like Langston Hughes, Coles is always willing to give a little more to the profession and the race.

Coles has unmistakably woven his drive for equality, opportunity, and love and concern into the social and architectural fabric of Buffalo. In the 1960's Coles came to Buffalo to implement his MIT master's thesis, "A study for the revitalization of the Historic Ellicott District" in the rapidly deteriorating urban core of Buffalo. Importantly, he has done it with sensitivity, care, and commitment few architects could equal. He has infused his local vision of Buffalo with a vitality and creativity that makes a strong statement for the African-American architect in both Western New York and across the country. He has extended his efforts, energies, and effectiveness to the future, affecting architects of tomorrow with his involvement. If the Black architect is in fact moving off the endangered list, it is due in large part to the efforts of architects such as Robert Traynham Coles, who have done so much to enriched our environment and continue the "circle."

Dr. Richard K. Dozier, AIA
Professor, School of Architecture
Florida Agricultural and Mechanical University

---

1. Adams, Michael. "A Legacy of Shadows." Progressive Architecture. February, 1991. 85-87.

2. See "The Practice of Architecture in a Post-Industrial City: The profile of a Black Architect-An Endangered Species." University of Kansas Lecture, Robert Coles, March 28, 1989.

3. It was Evans who presented Coles' thesis design for a community center and recreational faculty to the Ellicott District Urban Renewal and Development Authority.

4. Coles often quotes Langston Hughes' term "endangered species" which refers to African-American architects.

Introduction

As I end fifty years of practice as an architect, I can truly say that it has been my life and a positively satisfying one. When I was growing up, there was only one Black architect in my city, and he was not allowed to practice as a true professional. Had he lived fifty years later, he might have benefited from the opportunities opening in the profession.

I did not pick architecture by accident. I had wanted to follow my older brother into a different course of study but was shunted into building design rather than architecture. I took to design like a duck takes to water; and when my teacher showed me what architects did, I knew that was what I wanted to be. Several weeks later, he took me aside and told me that there were no Black architects, and suggested that I look elsewhere for an occupation. Undiscouraged, I resolved to be an architect and one of the best.

After high school, I spent two years at the college my parents had attended, Hampton Institute, and then transferred to the University of Minnesota, a large state school in the Midwest. Of the two hundred and fifty students enrolled in architecture, I was the only Black. I went on for my Masters at the Massachusetts Institute of Technology, which was the high point of my academic career. In my graduate year at MIT, in 1955, I won the Rotch Traveling Scholarship, awarded by the Boston Society of Architects, which allowed my wife and me to spend almost a year in Europe.

Always concerned about the neighborhood I grew up in Buffalo,

Robert Traynham Coles working on plans for the Joseph J. Kelly Gardens housing complex, c. 1963.

(Reproduction by permission of the Buffalo & Erie County Public Library, Buffalo, NY)

I had designed a recreation center for that neighborhood for my Master's thesis. In 1960, I was asked to use that design for the $1.5 million John F. Kennedy Recreation Center, located in the Ellicott District. That initial commission led to starting my own practice in 1963.

Since then, I have always focused on the have-nots rather than the haves. During the 1960s and 1970s, I led community efforts to improve the social, political and economic conditions of minorities in Buffalo, founding the East Side Community Organization in 1964 and spearheading the drive which raised $150,000 to bring Saul Alinsky and the Industrial Areas Foundation to Buffalo to organize the Black community. I was instrumental in founding the Community Planning Assistance Center (CPAC) of Western New York in 1970, and in 1973 I helped form the statewide Association of Community Design Development Centers. In 1974, I joined the national AIA staff as Deputy Vice President for Minority Affairs, to ensure greater minority participation in the architectural profession.

When I returned to my own practice in 1976, I continued to promote relationships between potential clients and minority firms. During my practice, I hired nearly thirty women and minorities—my own effort to make the practice look more like the society we serve.

In 1967 I led a group of community leaders in organizing the Committee for an Urban Campus. We hoped to sway the efforts in determining the future location of the new campus for the University of Buffalo in favor of a location on the city's waterfront. As a Buffalonian, I continue to be concerned with the welfare of its citizens, and particularly its minority population. One of the proudest achievements of my career was the completion in 2006 of the Merriweather Library, designed to serve the east-side community in which it is located.

My good friend and college classmate, R. Randall (Randy) Vosbeck, wrote a book about his firm, *Design Matters*, about five years ago and suggested I use it as the basis for my own book. Thanks to Randy, I went on to complete this book.

Robert Traynham Coles, FAIA
2016

Architect Robert Traynham Coles stands behind a model of his first project – the John F. Kennedy Recreation Center at Clinton and Hickory Streets – in the exhibition of his work in the Buffalo & Erie County Historical Society Museum, May, 2002.

Photo: Ronald J. Colleran/The Buffalo News

Chapter 1:
Influences and Opportunities

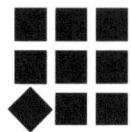

Robert Traynham Coles once told a reporter interviewing him about his career as an architect, "I go to play daily; it's not work for me." In over 50 years since Coles founded his firm in Buffalo, NY, his love for his chosen profession has helped shape his hometown's built environment and that of cities across the country, not to mention their social and cultural landscapes. Some of Coles' designs in Buffalo have been cited as gems of the Mid-Century Modern style. Moreover, Coles has won respect and recognition well beyond Buffalo's borders, and has engaged with the profession in an ongoing dialogue to raise its commitment to inclusiveness and social justice. Fellow Buffalonian Dr. Richard Dozier, Dean Emeritus of the Robert Taylor School of Architecture & Construction Sciences at Tuskegee University has recently said of Coles, "few architects, period, have made the significant contributions to the profession" that he has.

While Coles may not have thought of it as work, establishing himself as a respected architect was not without struggle. He and his twin brother were born in Buffalo in 1929 to George E. Coles and Helena Coles, who had both been born in Virginia. His parents had both been educated at Hampton Institute (now Hampton University). His father was a postal worker in the railway mail service. Family tradition says that he was the first person from Buffalo drafted in World War I. His draft registration card, numbered 72, has the lower left corner torn off, indicating that he was to serve in a segregated, non-combat role. The family was the only African American family living in the predominantly blue collar, German-Catholic neighborhood called Cold Springs. The four Coles brothers, George Jr., Thomas, Robert and William, lived on the same block as Public School 8, which they all attended, where they all got into mischief and first experienced racism. In 2000, Coles reflected on his experience at PS 8, recalling that in the first grade his teacher cast him as the "Wild Man of Borneo" in the school play. On hearing about this, his mother promptly marched over to the school and told the teacher that no son of hers was going to play the "Wild Man of Borneo." It was an object lesson in standing up for his rights, and it eventually led him to early acts of advocacy.[†]

Architecture and advocacy have been the twin hallmarks of Robert Coles' long career. His experience as an advocate actually predated his commitment to architecture. He relates the story of going to Crystal Beach, Ontario in 1940, where he was told to use the "Colored" changing room. Afterward he wrote to the *Buffalo Evening News* detailing his experience, and urging the paper not to carry advertisements from the amusement park. Several weeks later, he recalls, the newspaper wrote him back and told him he should try the beach again. It was eleven year-old Coles' first act of advocacy.

After attending Public School 8, Coles enrolled at Buffalo's Technical High School, one of a dozen Black students in a class of over 300. He originally wanted to study engineering, but was placed in a building design course, intended to train students for jobs in the building trades rather than for professional positions. "I took to Building Design like a duck takes to water," he told an audience in 2001, "and

---

[†] George, Jr. the eldest of the Coles brothers, while still in Buffalo, enlisted in the Navy at the age of 17. Thomas followed him, joining the Army after he was graduated from Technical High School. Neither Robert nor William joined the armed forces. Thomas was killed in an automobile accident in 1951 while serving in Germany as an Army sergeant. William, who retired as a juvenile corrections worker for the State of Massachusetts, died of cancer in 1984. George, retired from the Navy with the rank of Lieutenant Commander. He died in 1997.

by the time I was a sophomore, I was leading my class and . . . decided that I wanted to be an architect." John Brent, Buffalo's first Black architect, designed the Michigan Avenue YMCA, a social and cultural center for Buffalo's Black community. However, he never had the opportunity to develop his own practice.

Coles found that the roadblocks that stymied Brent were still in place, but he was determined to overcome them. Despite his academic achievement (he eventually finished 3rd out of 300 in Technical High School's class of 1947), Coles was discouraged from pursuing his dream. He recalls that his teacher took him aside and told him "Bob, you're wasting your time trying to be an architect. There are no opportunities for Negroes in that area. Why don't you go to the Post Office, or become a social worker or a minister."

Many of his contemporaries went to work in factories after high school. Coles, however, had won the Alfred Hurrell Design Award when he was graduated, and using the proceeds to cover part of the expenses, he followed his parents' desire and enrolled at Hampton Institute. Coles did not feel sufficiently challenged academically at Hampton. In addition, he bridled at southern discrimination forcing him to sit in the back of the bus. He decided to transfer to the University of Minnesota in 1949, after the Buffalo Foundation awarded him an Edward H. Moeller scholarship. In the school of architecture he was the sole Black student in a class of 65 and a student body of 250.

While at Minnesota, he attended workshops led by R. Buckminster Fuller, noted for his futuristic geodesic domes. Encouraged by Fuller, he and other students, including R. Randall (Randy) Vosbeck, built their own geodesic dome over the course of two months. He also met Louis Angelikis, another student from Minneapolis. Working for Angelikis' father's firm, the pair co-designed the $350,000 Richfield State Bank in Richfield, Minnesota, completed in 1955.

Coles felt that the all-white faculty discriminated in grading. One incident, in particular, sticks out. After praising a design problem of Coles', a professor asked who did it. "When I raised my hand," he wrote later, the professor "said, 'oh,' and then graded me so low that I could not graduate with honors." Nevertheless, the friendships and associations he made at Minnesota were lasting influences on his career.

Noted architect, designer, and educator, Ralph Rapson, was another important Minnesota contact. Rapson was teaching at MIT at the time, but became Dean of the School of Architecture and Landscape Design at Minnesota shortly after Coles was graduated. Rapson was born with a congenital deformity that required the amputation of his right arm below the elbow. His ability to conquer this handicap and still produce beautiful designs and drawings inspired the young architecture student to confront his own challenge of racial discrimination.

Coles earned his Bachelor of Arts in 1951, followed by a Bachelor of Architecture degree in 1953. His experience at Minnesota shaped much of his subsequent career. He attended the university at the time that Whitney M. Young, Jr. was the director of the St. Paul Urban League, and he became a student activist in response to incidents like a 1953 Minneapolis Police stop. While walking home one night he was stopped by a white officer. Coles believes the fact that he was carrying his Eagle Scout badge saved him from being further harassed.

Coles organized a campus chapter of the NAACP, and led the chapter's successful campaign to have the university adopt a policy of non-discrimination in housing. Prior to the NAACP's campaign,

Richfield State Bank, Richfield, Minnesota, completed in 1955.
Photographer unidentified

the university housing bureau had kept records of off-campus landlords' preferences regarding their willingness to rent to African Americans, Jews, Roman Catholics, and other groups. As a result of the campaign, the university decided that such a policy condoned prejudice. It subsequently required all potential landlords registering with the bureau to agree to accept any registered student regardless of race or religion. Those failing to comply were removed from the registry and forbidden to rent to students.

Coles had already met Sylvia Meyn, the daughter of a midwestern Lutheran pastor and a school teacher, who was working in Minneapolis as a stenographer in 1952. The couple married in 1953, and Sylvia became Coles' essential, albeit at times reluctant, partner in business and the struggle for social justice. The young, interracial couple had already found themselves the subject of FBI surveillance, partly as a result of Coles' NAACP activity, an indicator of how intense and stressful that struggle would be.

With his new bride, Coles went on to MIT to continue his studies with Fuller and others. Coles was one of 20 students admitted to the graduate program that year, intending to "cap my education with a Master's degree so that I could teach." He has written that midway through the first year, the entire group of 20 international students "got bored studying Frederick Law Olmsted's Back Bay Fens." They invited Dean Pietro Belluschi and Graduate School Chairman, Lawrence Anderson, to a party, and requested that the school's leadership pick six well-known architects from a list of thirty and invite them each for a month's criticism of student work. Eero Saarinen, Louis Kahn,

Robert Traynham Coles (center) greets Ralph Rapson (left) and Tom Fisher (right). After meeting in the mid 1950s, Coles and Rapson became friends, and in later years Coles occasionally attended affairs in Minneapolis honoring Rapson, including this "Breakfast with Ralph" celebration in Minnesota in 2004.

Photographer unidentified

John Johansen, Minoru Yamasaki, Eduardo Catalando, and Paul Rudolph each came to MIT as a visiting critic, making for what Coles recalls as "a great semester". He also studied with Lawrence Anderson, head of the graduate program, and an early proponent of the International Style in the United States. Coles called Anderson "the most sensitive teacher" he ever had. He said that Anderson allowed him to freely express himself as an architect as he developed his own interest in modern architecture.

While Coles pursued his master's degree, he and Sylvia, now the parents of an infant son, Darcy, born in 1954, had to battle racism and housing discrimination in Boston and Cambridge, Massachusetts. He recalls walking with Sylvia one afternoon in 1954, when they were threatened by sailors in a passing car, apparently outraged by the sight of an interracial couple.

When they first moved to Boston, the Coles' easily obtained an apartment in North Cambridge on Chilton Street in a predominantly Black neighborhood. Upon returning from extended travel in Europe in 1956, however, their experience searching for housing was quite different. In a report titled "Housing Discrimination in the Boston Area:

Chapter 1: Influences and Opportunities   5

Robert and Syvia Coles, with their infant son, Darcy, in Ostia Lido, Italy, 1955.
Photo from the private collection of Robert and Sylvia Coles

Coles station wagon at Palazzo Saviate (Casa del Tourista), Rome, Italy, 1955.
Photo from the private collection of Robert and Sylvia Coles

A personal report of the experiences of Mr. and Mrs. Robert T. Coles, June-July, 1956," they detailed their experience looking for apartments that had been advertised for rent in the Harvard University housing registry and local newspapers. They were repeatedly told that apartments were available, then turned away when landlords met them and saw that Coles was Black. Only one explicitly said she "did not rent to colored." Most, instead said they would not rent to families with small children, or that the apartment had been rented to someone else in the interim between the Coles' calling and coming to see the accommodations. In every case they had originally been told that children were acceptable, they regularly found the apartments re-advertised after having been told that they were rented. They finally found an apartment in Cambridge.

The experience, the Coles' wrote, left them frustrated at "how humiliating it is to be shunned as tenants by their own countrymen." They found it ironic that they were denied freedom in choosing a place to live at the same time the State's General Court (state legislature) was debating whether to add the slogan "Cradle of Freedom" to Massachusetts' license plates. The couple subsequently took part in a class-action lawsuit to force the General Court to pass a non-discriminatory housing law. The law served as a model for other states. The experiences solidified Coles' commitment to social activism.

Coles received his Master of Architecture degree in 1955. His master's thesis, "Community Facilities in a Redevelopment Area—A Study and Proposal for the Ellicott District in Buffalo, NY," would later be crucial to launching his own firm in Buffalo and his life as an activist architect.

While studying at MIT, he entered a design competition for the Rotch Traveling Scholarship, sponsored by the Boston Society of Architects. The scholarship was established in 1883 to allow architectural students to travel abroad to visit great buildings of the past. Its goal is to stimulate the creative imagination of young architects, and to enrich their cultural knowledge. Scholarship juries are directed to "search for evidences of imaginative capacity" in the design projects submitted by competing students.

Many of the United States' most distinguished architects, including Louis Skidmore, Edward Durrell Stone, and Gordon Bunschaft, have been recipients.

Coles' entry, "A National Chain Roadside Restaurant," was the winning design, and he was awarded the 1955 scholarship. The $5,000 stipend allowed Coles to study architecture in Europe. He, Sylvia, and Darcy, traveled through ten countries, including Italy, Spain and France between October 1955 and May 1956. Shortly after returning to the United States, Coles' seven year old niece, Marion, whose father, Bob's older brother Thomas, had been killed in an automobile accident in Germany, came to live with the family. The Coles later adopted her.

The traveling experience gave Coles the opportunity to view first hand some of the greatest of European architecture, both historic and contemporary, at a time when European cities like Frankfurt, Hamburg and London were still rebuilding after the devastation of World War II. Meeting Europeans, and witnessing how they made decisions about rebuilding cities to allow people to comfortably live, work, and navigate urban spaces that reflected their culture was yet another factor shaping the rest of Coles' career.

Upon returning from Europe, Coles served internships and held junior positions that allowed him to further refine his philosophy of "civilizing urban spaces." He apprenticed first at the Boston firm of Perry, Shaw, Hepburn and Dean (1956-1957), the firm that rebuilt Colonial Williamsburg, and afterward at Boston's Shepley, Bulfinch, Richardson and Abbott, successor to H. H. Richardson, working on university and municipal buildings and recreational facilities.

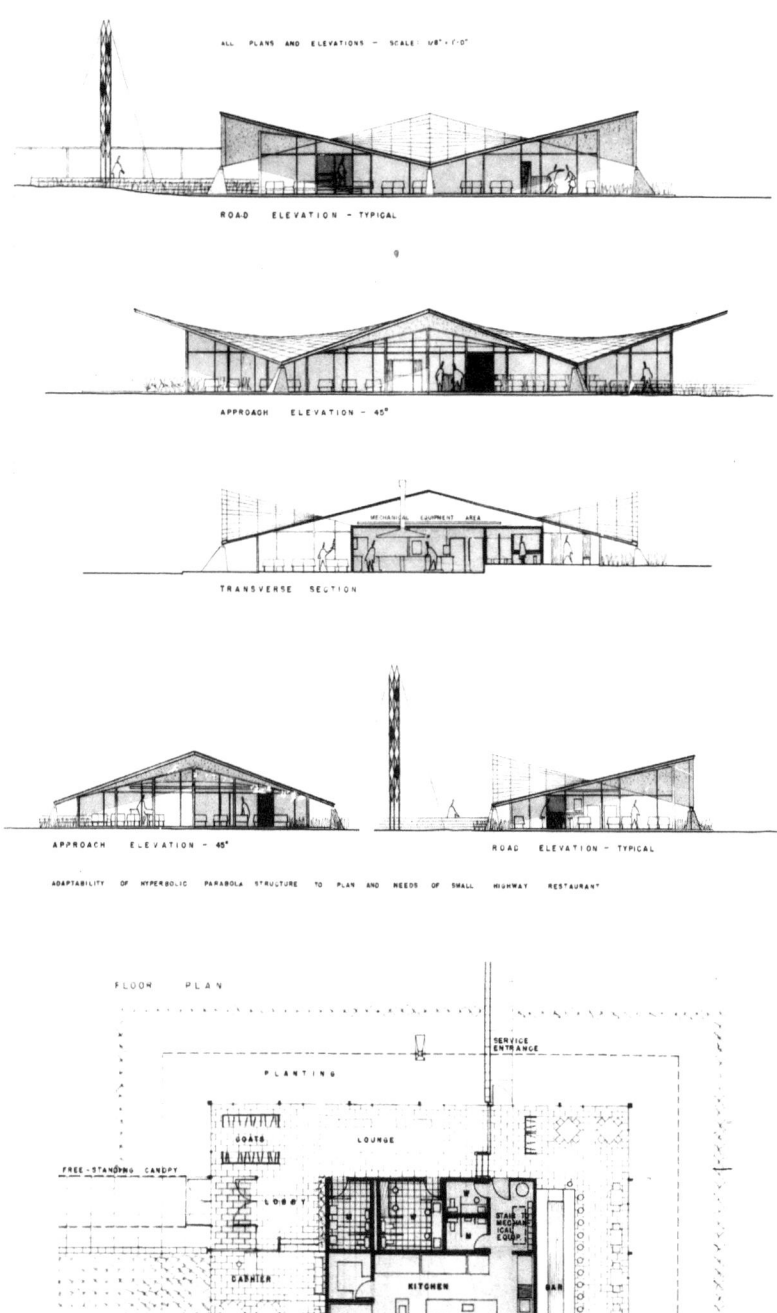

Coles' entry in the Final Competition for the 1955 Rotch Traveling Scholarship: "A National Chain Roadside Restaurant".

Drawings by Robert T. Coles

This house, designed by Robert Coles, was built with Techbuilt components. The goal set for the designers by the developers, Sterling Forest Corporation, was a house that would fit its surroundings and the existing contours of the land. The house was set 4 feet into the ground, so existing grades were barely disturbed. It has easy access to the outdoors from family and living areas, and it has plenty of glass to open it to views of lakes and forests. The exterior materials had natural finishes.   Photo from the private collection of Robert and Sylvia Coles

While at Perry, Shaw, Hepburn and Dean in 1957, Coles led a studio that included the Canadian-born architect, Frank Gehry. Gehry had taken the job in order to support his family while he was studying for an urban planning degree at Harvard, but decided to return to Los Angeles to join Victor Gruen's firm there before completing the degree.[†]

In 1958 Coles joined the Cambridge firm of Carl Koch and Associates as an architect. The association eventually led to his becoming Architect and Custom Design Manager for Techbuilt Homes (1959-1960). There he coordinated all architectural activities for the manufacturer of prefabricated components for Koch's "Techbuilt House" and other Koch designs. Despite his professional position and leadership role, racial discrimination persisted. For example, Coles relates, "In 1960, stopping at a restaurant for lunch while driving across Pennsylvania, my wife and I waited over a half hour to be served."

Nevertheless, as head of the Techbuilt architectural staff, Coles supervised the design and construction of over 200 residences on the eastern seaboard. Coles, himself, designed a number of residences, including one in Marblehead, Massachusetts that was cantilevered over a rocky ledge and rushing mountain stream. Clients included some notable individuals. Among these were Howard Koch and his wife, Anne, of Woodstock, NY. Koch wrote the 1938 radio script for "The War of the Worlds," which caused widespread panic through the East Coast, with people believing they were being invaded by Martians. Another Coles-designed residence, in Sterling Forest, NY, received an Award from Homes for Better Living in 1960.

Even more important than the specific buildings he designed was Coles' immersion in the Techbuilt system's innovative efforts to develop cost-effective technologies and designs providing affordable accom-

---

[†] Coles and Gehry stayed in touch for a time, and the Coles family briefly camped out on Gehry's living room floor when they visited Los Angeles during a cross-country camping trip in 1964. Coles saw Gehry again some years later when they both attended the American Institute of Architects (AIA) convention held in San Diego in 1977. He also recalls fondly Gehry's waving to him from the podium and mentioning their earlier association during a speech at the AIA Convention in Dallas in 1999.

After Coles saw Gehry at a later AIA convention, he proposed collaborating in the design competition announced by The National Museum of African American History and Culture in Washington in 2008. At first Gehry agreed, but had to bow out because he was caring for his daughter, Leslie, after she was stricken with the uterine cancer that claimed her life in December 2008. This was the last exchange between the two architects.

Robert and Sylvia Coles' residence at 321 Humboldt Parkway in Buffalo, completed in 1961. Black & white sculpture on the right is by Jack Solomon. The home was placed on the *National Register of Historic Places*, in 2011.   Photo: L. Kagelmacher

modations in post-World War II America. Techbuilt systems contributed significantly to what is now known as the Mid-Century Modern style. The style features structures with ample windows and open floor plans, and blurs the distinction between "outside" and "inside." Moreover, its then-groundbreaking post and beam construction eliminated bulky support walls in favor of walls that could be made largely of glass, or be opaque when necessary. The style's flexibility, relative inexpensiveness, and efficiency fit perfectly with Coles' evolving vision of creating affordable, livable, functional residential and public buildings in urban areas. It served him well for the rest of his career.

His future in the Boston area seemed secure in 1960. He was already designing a home for his family in Cambridge when in 1960 a telephone call from Clinton B.F. Brill of Buffalo changed his life. William L. Evans, Director of the Buffalo Urban League, himself trained as an architect, had suggested Coles' thesis design to the Ellicott District Urban Renewal and Development Authority. The architectural and engineering firm of DeLeuw, Cather and Brill received the commission to build the Ellicott District Recreation Center, later renamed the John F. Kennedy Recreation Center, the subject of his Master's thesis, and asked Coles to come to Buffalo for three months to help get the project underway. On the advice of Lawrence Anderson, who told him that "the right to come to Cambridge to get an education is coupled with the obligation to return to the hinterland and use it," Coles accepted the offer. Three months became six, and eventually the firm hired Coles to head all of its architectural design operations at the Buffalo office.

At the beginning of the project Coles commuted between Cambridge and Buffalo, but after a year decided to move back to his home town. He revised the plans for the Cambridge house, building, instead, on a lot on Humboldt Parkway on Buffalo's east side. The site was in the Black middle class Hamlin Park neighborhood, part of Frederick Law Olmsted's park and parkway system, which faced serious disruption at the time. The broad, park-like median and gracious shade trees that had characterized the street were slated to be torn out to

Chapter 1: Influences and Opportunities   9

be replaced by a multi-lane expressway to facilitate automobile travel between downtown Buffalo and the suburbs. When completed, the project slashed a quiet, charming residential neighborhood in two.

Coles told a reporter in 2010 that in his practice he specialized in projects that provided positive influences to a community. His own home was an early example. He set about designing a house and studio that would take advantage of the expressway without sacrificing the opportunity for a quiet, comfortable, neighborhood lifestyle. When the house and studio complex was nominated to the *National Register of Historic Places*, the application cited the home's orientation as one of its most significant features. Unlike traditional buildings in the neighborhood that face the street and feature large porches, the Coles house and studio turns its back on the street and expressway. The public space of the studio, largely without windows, fronts the street, while "the residence is oriented with its façade facing the quiet, tranquil rear court, where the din from the expressways is hardly heard."

It was an early demonstration of how Coles' architecture could create a positive urban experience, even in difficult circumstances. The home was completed in 1961, and Coles later told a reporter, "Frankly, I think it is the best thing I ever did." It was placed on the *National Register of Historic Places* in 2011 as "an excellent example of mid-twentieth century Modern residential architecture that incorporated some pre-fabricated and pre-cut components into its construction."

Coles' own experience, crystallized by his studies and European travel had already caused him to think about civilizing urban spaces. He has often articulated that goal, calling on architects to be "revolutionaries who see their architecture as a broad movement to enhance the quality of life of urban people." Many of his ideas were given physical shape in the Kennedy Recreation Center, bounded by Clinton, Pine, Hickory and South Division Streets in Buffalo. Remembering how John Brent's Michigan Avenue YMCA served Buffalo's African American community as a cultural and artistic center as well as a recreational facility, Coles incorporated spaces in the new complex to support senior citizen activities, scout troops, and theatre and arts groups. A well-baby clinic was part of the design, along with recreational facilities including children's game rooms and a television lounge. When completed, the building demonstrated Coles' philosophy, later articulated more fully in both writing and construction, that private spaces should become smaller in urban society as public spaces, facilitating interaction, become larger.

Western New York Heritage magazine included the John F. Kennedy Recreation Center in an article titled "Western New York's Unsung Architectural Gems" in 2013. Buffalo architect, Clinton Brown, FAIA, notes that the building has "stood the test of time, both architecturally and functionally." The design, Brown wrote, "clearly and cleanly expresses characteristic modern structural, formal, functional and, yes, decorative features in cast-in-place and pre-cast concrete, glass, glass block and stone, with nicely balanced interplays of straight and curved shapes and smooth and rough surfaces."

Brown also concludes that the building is clearly a product of a particular time in American history, a time in which Americans believed that by "creating beautiful and orderly places," the federal government could help ameliorate the lives of urban residents living in blighted neighborhoods, and give them hope for the future.

Coles' 321 Humboldt Parkway home from the backyard Photo: Gerard Myers

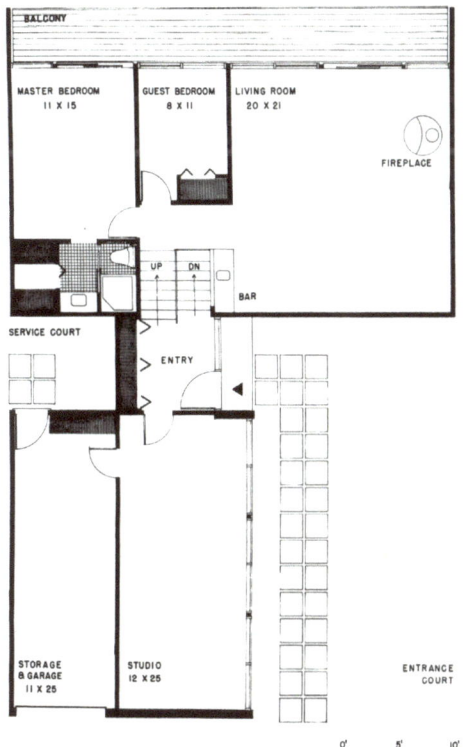
321 Humboldt Parkway, upper floor plan

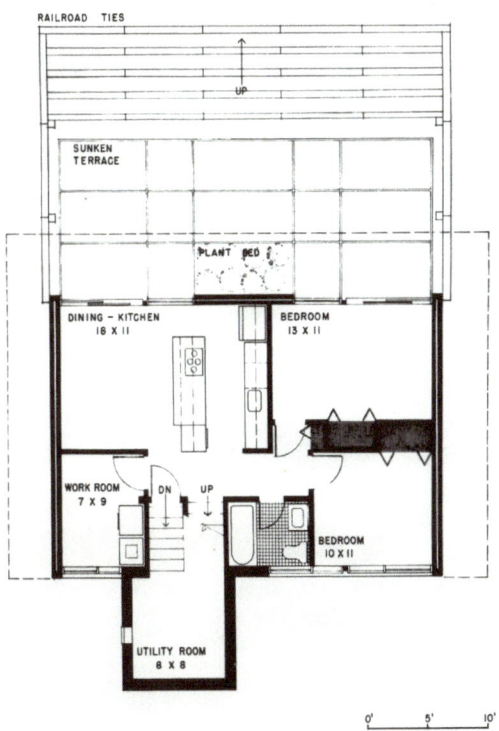
321 Humboldt Parkway, lower floor plan

Chapter 1: Influences and Opportunities 11

The John F. Kennedy Recreation Center in Buffalo, NY, Coles' first project after returning to Buffalo in the early 1960s. See project description, Appendix C, page 64. Photos above and below: Gerard Myers

View from inside the multi-purpose room of the John F. Kennedy Recreation Center

Chapter 2:
The Firm: Founding and Philosophy

After completing the John F. Kennedy Recreation Center, Coles opened his own firm in Buffalo in 1963. Offices were originally in the Coles home on Humboldt Parkway, with Sylvia serving as secretary and bookkeeper. Incorporated as a Professional Corporation in 1971, at the time of its dissolution in December 2012, it was the oldest African American-owned architecture firm in New York and the northeast.

Coles had particular goals for the business. Of course, one was to design urban spaces that reflected his philosophy. That philosophy emphasized thoroughly understanding the urban dwellers, many of whom were Black, and the problems they faced. Only then, he argued, could the architect be "a conceptionist who will lead our citizens into a better urban world." He told a young architecture student in the mid-1960s that architecture is an urban art, and that to be successful the student needed to immerse himself in the social issues of the city and its people before he thought about designing buildings.

Speaking at Hampton Institute in 1968, Coles told a group of architecture school faculty that the "profession must reconsider giving awards for good design and stress good livability." Respecting the values of urban dwellers was crucial to an architect with the legitimate goal of revitalizing urban areas "so that [citizens] may live in a more stimulating environment tomorrow." In a 1981 article in *Buffalo Spree* magazine, [see "The Impact of an Architect: Robert Coles", Appendix E, page 97] Buffalo journalist Linda Levine observed that even Coles' office reflected the architect's philosophy in that his own office was small, while a "shared central space is generous."

Coles' commitment to cities is unwavering. After the attacks on the World Trade Center in 2001, he was appalled by those who thought that functions that cities and high rise buildings accommodated should be dispersed. "Those who have those views have forgotten that our cities are the greatest creations of mankind," he wrote. "They are the centers of our arts and our culture and our industries," he continued. Perhaps their most civilizing role, he argued, is that "[t]hey are where we can have the greatest diversity—all shades of black and white, Asian, Caribbean—the greatest opportunities for education and employment, and in our age, recreation." He concluded: "In destroying the World Trade Center, let us hope that the terrorists have not destroyed our faith in our cities, and the joy of our architecture." Coles' commitment to guaranteeing that everyone has equal access to the benefits of urban living is as unwavering as his love of cities.

Coles first articulated many of his thoughts about historic preservation and community revitalization in "An Architect Looks at Buffalo", in 1963 [reprinted in Appendix E, page 91]. Central to his thoughts was the notion of creating humane public spaces. That meant, among other things, celebrating the waterfront, and providing pedestrian access to beautiful, inspirational spaces. Among those spaces he cited Shelton Square, Arlington Park and, above all, the Olmsted parks and parkways. "Will we ever realize that the city and the automobile are incompatible?" he asked, arguing that more expressways and parking ramps destroyed neighborhoods and drove people from the city.

Implicit in his criticism of automobiles and downtown parking garages was advocacy of user-friendly public transportation. He warned his readers against "mistaking newness for goodness," and cautioned against attempts to suburbanize the city through residential architecture based on individual frame houses. "One wonders," he mused, "whether it might be better for Buffalo or any city to rehabilitate what it already has to attract its former residents back into the city, rather than to build at tremendous cost new towers on the horizon in the midst of blight and deterioration." This was a manifesto of an architect determined to civilize urban spaces for the people who lived in them.

He expanded on some of his ideas while talking to *Buffalo Courier-Express* columnist, Virginia Dell in 1965. He commented that Buffalo was largely a late 19th- and early 20th-century city built primarily of wood, and that "no city in history meant to last was built of wood." While Buffalo was a city that invited

Solomon Court, Buffalo, NY, 1968. Materials in the court were simple red brick paving, redwood boards, and redwood fencing to act as a backdrop for the various works by the sculptor. Located in the heart of an artists community which sponsored an annual festival, the court served as a focal point for many community events. Photo: Gerard Myers

rebuilding, Coles lamented some decisions being made about how to do it. Downtown buildings that were well built and had character, he complained, were being razed in favor of relatively modern structures, but "people are trying to save wooden housing that is not worth saving." He continued "that doesn't make sense in terms of housing for future generations." Instead, Coles contended that "people have to be ready to accept a different system of living . . . the single family house on a single lot is an inconsistency in the city."

In order to provide housing that was affordable for people who needed it, Coles looked to new technologies to provide "new, expandable systems of housing . . . to meet future needs." The technological advances, he told his Hampton audience in 1968, could provide decent housing for millions of people at a fraction of the then prevailing construction costs. He challenged architects to be

Joseph J. Kelly Gardens housing complex. See project description, Appendix C, page 67. Photo: Gerard Myers

Paul Lindsay Sample Memorial Playground, Chautauqua, NY. See project description, Appendix C, page 68.
Paul Maze/Phototech

leaders in the technological revolution, but lamented that neither they nor the building materials industry were moving in that direction.

Like his own home and studio, the award-winning Joseph J. Kelly Gardens housing complex for the elderly in Buffalo, completed in 1967, was a relatively early attempt to put this philosophy into practice. The AIA Homes for Better Living Competition recognized the project with an Honorable Mention in 1968. Buffalo architect Theodore Lownie has commented that at the time, public housing was "immediately recognizable." It was high-rise, massive, institutional, and forbidding. "Bob changed all that," he said. In contrast to other projects of the era, "the buildings were on a residential scale that fit into the surrounding residential neighborhood. They had generously-sized rooms, and pleasant surroundings. No one else was building public housing like that back then."

Residence for Mr. and Mrs. Gerald Berlyn, Worcester, Massachusetts, 1965. Drawing by Robert T. Coles

Among the firm's other early projects were the Townsend Dental Clinic, the Paul Lindsay Sample Memorial Playground at the Chautauqua Institution in Chautauqua, NY, and a sculpture court in Buffalo. Sample Memorial Playground was Coles' first collaboration with Jack Solomon, a Buffalo automobile mechanic with a bent for creating imaginative steel plate sculptures with a cutting torch. Coles designed the playground as a circular concrete form, tilted like a saucer that Solomon filled with colorful steel forms, including a slide. A raised ramp allowed parents to supervise children while enjoying a view of Chautauqua Lake. The New York State AIA awarded the project a Design Citation in 1968.

Solomon later commissioned Coles to develop what became Solomon Court, wrapped around Solomon's home near the corner of Elmwood Avenue and Allen Street in Buffalo's Allentown

Weekend house in Attica, NY, for Drs. Lydia Wright and Frank Evans, 1968. Drawing by Robert T. Coles

Residence for Mr. and Mrs. Charles Eppolito, Orchard Park, NY, 1971. Drawing by Robert T. Coles

neighborhood. Coles described it as "a unique public open space with entrances marked by trees on Elmwood and Allen Streets." It featured a raised stage that could be used for concerts, presentations, or as a display platform for Solomon's sculpture.

Other early projects including a number of private residences, in Worcester, Massachusetts; and Grand Island, Attica, Ellicottville and Orchard Park, in New York, were also designed and built between 1966 and 1971. All reflect Coles' style and design philosophy that emphasize creating humane public spaces, livable private spaces, and using affordable, flexible systems to meet clients' needs. The Worcester, Massachusetts residence for Mr. and Mrs. Gerald Berlyn, constructed in 1965, the weekend house for Dr. Lydia Wright and Dr. Frank Evans, in Attica, NY, (1968), and the house for Mr. and Mrs. Charles Eppolito in Orchard Park, NY (1971), like all of Coles' residential designs, according to Clinton Brown,

share a similar, minimalistic, Scandinavian-inspired modernist design, utilizing natural materials, including wood and stone. While varying in form and configuration, [they] all share a compact, simple and functional design that minimizes wasted space and incorporates storage and utility spaces efficiently within the building without a traditional basement or attic.

Despite his success with residential designs, following the completion of the Orchard Park residence, Coles decided that the time and effort in consulting with private clients would be better spent in designing public buildings and involvement in social causes.

In 1968, despite his opposition to locating the SUNY Buffalo campus in Amherst (see below), the State University Construction Fund selected Coles to design the new campus' Health, Physical Education and Recreation Complex (HPER). Also, there were reports that R. Buckminster Fuller's firm might partner with him on the project.

Coles, having known Fuller from both Minnesota and MIT, attended the 1967 Montreal World's Fair, and was thrilled to see the United States Pavilion designed by

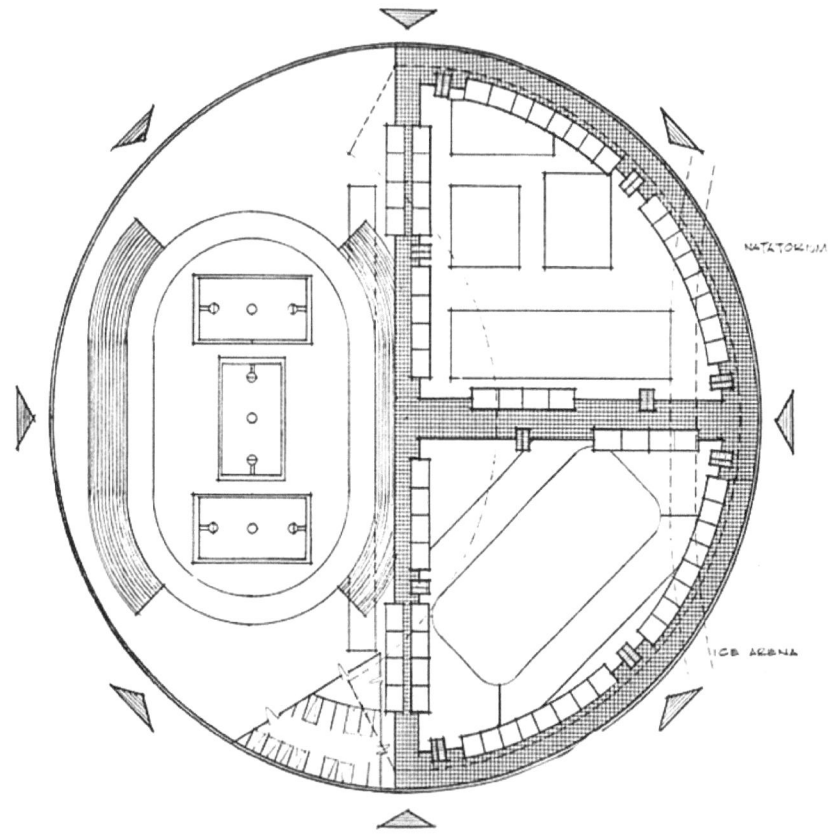

Buckminster Fuller's proposed physical education complex for UB, drawn by Charles Rush, Jr.

Chapter 2: The Firm: Founding and Philosophy   17

Fuller and his Cambridge partner, Shoji Sadao. With the urging of Buffalo banker Lewis G. Harriman, Coles contacted Fuller regarding the possibility of their collaborating on a domed stadium for the National Football League Buffalo Bills. While Fuller and Sadao were enthusiastic, that project never materialized. Coles' next contact with Fuller was at a Toronto press conference in 1968, when Fuller presented a visionary proposal to link downtown Toronto and its waterfront with a series of tetrahedral structures.

Toronto did not adopt the plan, but his contact with Fuller at the press conference encouraged Coles to propose a collaboration with him on the SUNY physical education complex. According to Coles, Fuller was very enthusiastic about the project and developed a cogent philosophical statement about the importance of the facility. Fuller envisioned a total envelope scheme to enclose the entire complex under a single roof. The State University Construction Fund staff, to Coles' dismay, "lacked the creative insights to appreciate Fuller." When his scheme was rejected, Fuller withdrew from the project. In Fuller's 1969 letter of withdrawal, he told the Construction Fund that his departure would allow Coles the opportunity to "introduce a cultural phase of dark-skinned competence paralleling the athletic experience. Architecture is the place to do it."

When Fuller and Sadao bowed out, Coles added staff to tackle the work himself. Charles Rush, Jr., Mel Alston, an African American architectural student, and Ed Norris, a Black architect and a colleague of Coles' from Boston, joined the firm. Although the Health, Physical Education, and Recreation Complex project was unexpectedly halted in 1969 because of lack of funding, other contracts for low income housing and neighborhood health facilities in Buffalo and Rochester, renovations to a building at Buffalo State College, and a new school required additional new staff in 1969.

After incorporating in 1971, with Coles as sole shareholder, President and Treasurer, and Sylvia as Corporate Secretary, Coles moved his offices to leased space at 1151 Main Street in Buffalo. A staff of between fifteen and twenty supervised the various projects under contract.

The firm's expansion helped Coles serve a wider purpose, too, to recruit and mentor African Americans and women in the practice of architecture in a way that had never been available to him as a young professional. As early as 1968, in his speech at Hampton, Coles publicly lamented the absence of African Americans in the profession. "Out of 200 registered architects in the Buffalo metropolitan area, I am the only [African American]," he told the audience, continuing that according to the 1960 census, only 33 black registered architects practiced in New York. A staff photograph from the early 1970s shows how committed Coles was to redressing that imbalance. It pictures a diverse group of African Americans, a Chinese American, an Egyptian, and Nigerian, Polish and Estonian Americans, men and women pursuing a common goal.

Coles once said that he saw himself not as a Black architect, but as an architect who was Black. In the firm's early years, Coles described himself as an architect by day, activist by night. He defined "activist" in 1968 as someone engaged in "the active leadership in the political and social sphere, regardless of how unpopular the issue may be." An activist "must be the initiator of new plans for the community, rather than simply the effector."

Riots in nearby Rochester in 1964, and in Watts in 1965 reaffirmed Coles' conviction that American cities, Buffalo in particular, needed improved schools, housing, streets and neighborhoods. More and more his architecture and activism became one and the same. He advocated grass-roots organization to mobilize political power to alleviate physical blight. Born of the Civil Rights activism of the early 1960s, Coles' firm both anticipated and facilitated the changes that swept urban America in the late 1960s and early 1970s.

In the early 1970s, Coles' firm had its offices at 1151 Main Street. This photograph from 1972 shows the diverse group of men and women who staffed the various projects under contract at that time. Photo: Gerard Myers

Back row, left to right: Casimir Acholonu, Mel Alston, Van Johnson
2nd row, left to right: Samuel Fenston, CPA, Richard Chalmers, Aly El-Tobgy, Gene Holzerland, Robert West, Ed Brodzinsky, Sylvia Coles, Charles E. Rush, Robert Coles, Ike Krzywinski, Warren Ansley
Front row, left to right: Viestarts Racenis, Ho Kim, Weanette James, Sharon Jackson, Betty Kaufman

Richard Prosser and Robert Traynham Coles, c. 1970.   Photo: Sylvia Coles

Chapter 3:
An Activist Matures

Commenting in 1973, Coles attributed much of his firm's early success to the "growth in political power in the black community." Much of that growth locally was the direct result of Coles' activism outside the firm. The success of those activities also brought local and national push-back that sent Coles' professional career in new directions.

In 1964 Coles met The Rev. Richard Prosser, a Presbyterian minister and associate of community organizer and social activist Saul Alinsky. Prosser had come from Chicago to Lackawanna, NY, to be executive director of Friendship House, a settlement house in the Steel City. He commissioned Coles to design a new building for the organization.

The building incorporated many of the ideas Coles had worked out for his own home. Set in a blighted urban area, it faced inward on a large, landscaped courtyard that could be viewed from spacious window walls that also admitted light to the building's interior. It was another example of "creating beautiful and orderly places," to ameliorate the lives of urban residents and give them hope.

In 2013, local residents remembered fondly the activities at the center. The *Buffalo News*, reported that in its heyday, it was "a hub of activity in the city's 1st Ward, hosting an array of human service programs, a food pantry, a foster care program and a summer camp." Unfortunately, a costly legal settlement in 1997 forced the center to close.

It stood abandoned and deteriorated until it was finally condemned in 2007. It was torn down after the City of Lackawanna appropriated funds for demolition in 2013.

Probably even more important than the opportunity to design the building was the impact that Prosser had on Coles' overall understanding of his profession. "It was [Prosser]," Coles commented later, "who brought out the advocacy that was buried inside me." Prosser's experience also helped show the architect how to turn advocacy into action.

Prosser received the AIA's 1986 Whitney M. Young, Jr. Citation posthumously "in recognition of a significant contribution to social responsibility." Coles demonstrated his indebtedness to Prosser's influence by writing the nomination. In it, he noted that Prosser helped create "an organization that developed more than 100 new homes for modest-income persons in deteriorating downtown neighborhoods, and he helped initiate a commercial medical complex that became a catalyst for inner-city development." Moreover, he "helped establish a national network of community design centers, and was a founding director, vice president and president of the National Community Design Center organization. His greatest contribution", the nomination went on "was the involvement of students who interacted with inner-city residents and organizations to help shape the inner-city neighborhoods; these students in turn were shaped by the forces they tried to resolve." From the mid 1960s to the

The courtyard of the new Friendship House. Richard Prosser, the director, commissioned Robert Coles to design the building. See project description, Appendix C, page 66. Photo: Gerard Myers

Robert Coles (in tee-shirt) talking with Al Tinney, jazz pianist (with hat and tan jacket) at Buffalo's Juneteenth Festival.
Photo: Sylvia Coles

mid 1970s Prosser involved Coles in many of those efforts with dramatic results.

In the 1960s, America's cities—Newark, Detroit, Los Angeles—were burning because inner-city African Americans felt that they were being left out of the prosperity that majority whites were enjoying. In 1964 when nearby Rochester, home of Xerox and Kodak, exploded in one of the worst race riots in the nation, Buffalo began to take notice. Coles took an active part in a variety of efforts to right the wrongs.

In the early 1960s he served on the US Civil Rights Commission's Western New York Area Subcommittee for the Study of Discrimination in the Medical Profession. The committee's research and advocacy brought an end to segregated hospital wards in Western New York. He also continued to target some of the root causes of urban unrest.

To further the goal of revitalizing Buffalo's neighborhoods and insure their viability, Richard Prosser suggested that the Industrial Areas Foundation, headed by community organizer Saul Alinsky, who was working to develop grassroots organizations in both Rochester and Syracuse, be hired to organize Buffalo's African American community. Prosser, who had worked with Alinsky in the Northwest Community Organization in Chicago, contacted Alinsky, and he accepted. Alinsky came to Buffalo in 1964, met Coles, Prosser, and Professor Jesse E. Nash, Jr., a Canisius College sociologist who later became head of Buffalo's Model Cities program. Alinsky outlined his program, which required a commitment from the community.

Alinsky returned to Buffalo in January 1965 for a meeting at the Michigan Avenue YMCA, attended by several dozen people. He explained that his organization would need $150,000 for the effort. The local group decided to form the East Side Community Organization (ESCO) to raise the funds. Rev. Richard D. Ford, a Presbyterian minister who headed a local settlement house, was elected President, Coles Vice-President, and Dr. Lydia T. Wright, a pediatrician and Buffalo Board of Education member, Trustee. Sylvia Coles was pressed into service as the organization's Secretary and Treasurer.

ESCO's fund drive succeeded in raising the necessary $150,000,

ESCO Vice-President Robert T. Coles with Board Trustee Dr. Lydia T. Wright, Saul Alinsky, and Rev. Richard D. Ford, ESCO President. Photo taken during Alinsky's 1965 Buffalo visit (photographer unidentified).

the bulk coming from various Protestant denominations. In 1967, Alinsky returned to Buffalo for a gala celebration, and Richard Harmon, from Chicago, was named as the local organizer. His task was to listen to grievances from the African American community and to find creative ways to address them. To coordinate the efforts of 90 or more community groups, organizers formed BUILD (Build Unity, Independence, Liberty and Dignity).

One of BUILD's primary objectives was education, and it pressured the Board of Education to create new models for effective schools. Dr. Wright worked with the Board of Education to create the BUILD Academy. Founded in 1969, it was originally an elementary school with high academic standards and an enrollment that was 53% Black and 47% White. A curriculum including Black history and culture, as well as a program of improved guidance counseling characterized the school. Unlike any other school in the Buffalo system, the Academy had parental and community involvement as a chief goal. To realize that goal, the school was originally governed by a board consisting of representatives from the African American community, Buffalo State College, and Associate School Superintendent Eugene Reville. When it opened, the school enrolled students in grades K through 4, later expanding to include grades 5 through 8. Along with the Juneteenth Festival, held in Buffalo every June, the school is among BUILD's most important legacies.

Recognizing the need to develop alliances with the majority population, BUILD organizers also created a sister organization, CAUSE (Coalition for Action, Unity and Social Equality) with initial funding of $50,000 that Coles helped raise. Like BUILD, CAUSE pressed the Board of Education to create a new school. Carol Hoyt, a community activist and wife of New York State Assemblyman Bill Hoyt, worked with the west side community to create the CAUSE School, a short-lived elementary school with a strong focus on social justice and experimental education.

In his firm's early years, Coles also took a leadership role in the controversy surrounding the location of the new campus of the State University at Buffalo (UB). In 1966, the State University was planning to build the new campus in suburban Amherst, NY, following a de-

Chapter 3: An Activist Matures 23

Whitney M. Young, Jr., keynote speaker at 1968 AIA convention in Portland, Oregon. Public domain photo

cision made by university trustees in 1964. After about three weeks of study, Buffalo's Planning Board appealed that decision to Governor Nelson A. Rockefeller, who, in August urged the State University of New York system's President, Samuel B. Gould, to conduct a study of an alternative site on the Buffalo waterfront. Rockefeller cited the benefits of a location in the heart of the city "mutually advantageous to the students of the university and the residents of the city."

Following a decision to restudy the waterfront site, a group of prominent Buffalo citizens organized the Committee for an Urban University to promote the concept. Coles was named chairman of the committee. A fierce advocate for urban living, he had already expressed amazement that the city ignored the waterfront's potential. "We cannot but wonder," he wrote in "An Architect Looks at Buffalo" in 1963, "why a city so blessed with such a splendid natural setting has literally turned away from what should be its greatest asset." [See full article, reprinted in Appendix E, page 91.] Other officers included investment banker Donald Ross, banker Lewis G. Harriman, Jr., Graphic Controls Corporation President Max B. E. Clarkson, UB School of Social Work Professor Marvin Bloom, and University at Buffalo Medical School Professor Dr. Harry Sultz. Others active on the committee were journalist Douglas Turner, attorney Carl Green, the Rev. Richard Prosser, and Dr. Lydia T. Wright. Coles later wrote that "Max [Clarkson] was the heart of the committee and I was the soul."

"Max and our committee," Coles remembered in 1998, "managed, in August 1966, to get Governor Nelson Rockefeller to stop planning on the University. It was an election year and the Governor wasn't interested in having any controversy standing in his way to re-election." The State called on Dr. Mason Gross, President of Rutgers University, to arbitrate.

One local newspaper reported that a waterfront site for the campus "could be Downtown's salvation." Another reported that, toward that end, the Committee for an Urban University had "dedicated itself to developing additional complementary resource material and influences leading to the selection of the downtown waterfront area."

In October 1966 Coles addressed the Campus Planning Committee, a group of people interested in the direction the new UB campus was going to take. Its primary concerns were the location of the new campus and the role of students and faculty in planning the campus wherever it was built.

"Max [Clarkson] was our major presenter in the public hearings that were held in early 1967," Coles recalled, but "as eloquent as Max was, we couldn't persuade Mason Gross," who in February reaffirmed the decision to move the University to Amherst. Linda Levine wrote in 2002 that "Coles saw the University as the only thing that could have

Standing outside the CPAC headquarters in Buffalo: Janet Prosser, unidentified, Cleon Service (CPAC President) in doorway, Richard Prosser, Robert Traynham Coles on right. Photographer unidentified

turned Buffalo around at that time." In a city "well past its prime as a heavy manufacturing and industrial center," he felt that a university with growing mission, scale and population could, in one decisive move, have provided a powerful replacement.

Coles' dream went unfulfilled, although years later, in the late 1980s, he continued his struggle over appropriate waterfront development as a member of the Horizons Waterfront Commission, established to facilitate comprehensive planning for Erie County's waterfront along Lake Erie. In 2002 Coles reflected with *Buffalo News* reporter, Tom Buckham, about his activities with the Committee for an Urban University, and the reporter concluded that Coles' "wide-ranging social activism, including his strident opposition in the 1960s to the construction of UB's new campus in Amherst—rather than on the Buffalo waterfront—may have hurt him professionally as much as his color." To this day Coles laments the decision to put the new campus in suburban Amherst, and sometimes ponders what might have been. Nevertheless, he reflected recently, "it created a dialogue about the role of a public university."

Coles attended his second AIA convention, held in Portland, Oregon in 1968, just two months after an assassin murdered Dr. Martin Luther King, Jr., igniting some of the worst looting and burning that American city centers had ever experienced. The keynote speaker at the convention was Whitney Young, Jr., executive director of the National Urban League, who castigated the architectural profession. Young squarely placed some of the blame for the turmoil on the profession, observing "I have to wonder about architects who design the 12- to 14-story vertical slums in our cities without restrooms on the basement floors, with recreation space for 10 kids when 5,000 live there." He concluded, "You are not a profession that has distinguished itself by your social and civic contributions to the cause of civil rights . . . . You are most distinguished by your thunderous silence and your complete irrelevance. . . . You are employers, you are key people in the planning of

Chapter 3: An Activist Matures 25

cities today. You share responsibility for the mess we are in—in terms of the white noose around the central city."

Young spoke from some experience with architecture and planning. Richard K. Dozier has suggested that Young's career had been significantly shaped by the spirit of African American architects. "It surrounded him as he grew up and went to school in buildings they had designed with pride," Dozier writes. Young's father, Whitney M. Young, Sr., was the first African American president of Lincoln Institute in Lexington, Kentucky, a campus largely designed by pioneer African American architect Vertner Woodson Tandy. Whitney Young, Jr. was born there in 1921. The future civil rights leader later attended Kentucky State Industrial College, and studied in buildings designed by Tandy's teacher, William Sidney Pittman.

Young had grown up and been inspired by environments designed by African American architects. Perhaps this was part of the reason for his frustration at the profession's insensitivity to minorities and to urban environments. His forthright speech in Portland, Dozier has written, "played a pivotal role in forcing the AIA and its members to rethink their role in community design and to look for ways to attract more young minorities into the field." Coles committed the rest of his career to furthering both of those goals.

The young architect returned to Buffalo more determined than ever to devote his practice to "urban architecture with special attention to buildings that relate to people," and realize his vision to revitalize Buffalo through neighborhood preservation programs. He also rededicated his efforts to serve as an example to young Blacks in the area and to provide the opportunity for apprenticeship to minority architecture students and graduates. Between 1963 and 2004, the firm employed nearly 30 minority and women architects and architectural interns.

In 1972, Coles, with Prosser and Charles Rush, Jr., founded the Community Planning Assistance Center (CPAC) to assist community groups in development projects. As noted above, Richard Prosser was a founding director, vice-president, and president of the National Community Design Center organization, based in Washington, DC, which created a model that involved students in interactions with inner city residents and organizations to help shape inner city neighborhoods. Rush, Coles' first intern architect, helped mobilize students in Western New York.

Coles also took his activism to a national level in 1972. With Robert Nash, Leon Bridges, and a dozen other Black architects, he was instrumental in forming the National Organization of Minority Architects (NOMA) that year, to address the concerns of Black architects. He reflected in 1981 that their clients were primarily homeowners and churches, as opposed to the corporate clients served by their white counterparts. "We were relegated to doing the black churches, the black social welfare facilities, or black housing developments, -- often on a shoestring budget" he wrote in a statement that largely reflected his own early career.

Coles and his fellow Black architects had attended the Portland convention "to let our fellow architects, who are 97% white male, know that we wanted a greater piece of the action." NOMA, he continued, "provided Black architects with an organized constituency to pressure the AIA to continue to implement the challenge of Whitney Young, and to encourage government agencies to adhere to the affirmative action requirements of the Federal Equal Opportunity statutes." Originally named the National Organization of Black Architects, the name was changed to embrace all minorities. Coles has said that NOMA was the most creative approach that African Americans have adopted to advance their place in the architectural profession. As a founding member, he initiated a newsletter sent to member firms, and also served as treasurer, secretary, and vice-president. Sylvia, too, played a key role assisting Bob with his various responsibilities at NOMA. Mindful of the significance of NOMA's activities, Coles placed his detailed records of NOMA correspondence and activities during his tenure as an officer in the Howard University research collection.

Other influential Black architects in NOMA became Coles' lifelong collaborators in his efforts to open the profession to minorities and women. These included NOMA founder and president, Robert Nash, from Washington, DC, a graduate of Howard University who specialized in schools and housing. Nash, a charismatic leader, served as president for two years at NOMA. Later he became the AIA's first African American vice-president. Another fellow NOMA activist was Wendell J. Campbell. Coles first met him in 1971 when they both attended the annual convention of the AIA in Detroit. While serving as the AIA's first Deputy Vice-President for Minority Affairs,

Coles helped prepare Campbell's application for the 1976 Whitney Young Award. Coles termed it a "labor of love," as he wove pieces of Campbell's life into the document that finally became the application. Campbell, who died in 2008, was remembered most for the opportunities he helped create and make possible for minority practitioners.

Between 1968 and 1974, in response to Whitney Young's criticism, the AIA recruited more Black members, and placed some in high positions. The organization established a minority architecture scholarship program. Other programs were aimed at elementary and secondary schools to identify prospective minority architecture students. Moreover, after Young's untimely death in 1971 in a swimming accident in Africa, the AIA established the Whitney M. Young, Jr. Award as a permanent reminder of the challenges that he articulated in 1968. However, progress ground to a halt with the recession of the early 1970s, and with policy decisions like Richard Nixon's 1973 moratorium on low and moderate income housing, a mainstay of Black architects' businesses. Some relief was provided by Gerald Ford's Secretary of Transportation, William Coleman, who served from 1975 to 1977. Coleman mandated that 15% of funds for mass transit must go to minority firms. The Reagan administration, however, dismantled remaining housing programs, and drastically reduced mass transit funding in the early 1980s.

William Thaddeus Coleman, US Secretary of Transportation, 1975-77.   Photo: Public Domain, Wikimedia Commons.

Above and below: State University of NY at Buffalo's Alumni Arena (c. 1982-85). See project description, Appendix C, pages 74-75. Photos: L. Kagelmacher

Chapter 4:
The Firm: New Challenges, New Directions

By late 1972 and early 1973, the recession and changes in public policy threatened Coles' thriving practice. It was typical in Black architectural firms at the time, that new private commissions did not make up for retrenchment in public projects. Coles was forced to reduce staff to himself and Ed Norris, give up the Main Street space, and move back to his home office. The strategies that Coles adopted to save the firm increasingly demonstrated the inseparability of his architecture and his activism.

Even when there was a possibility of participating in publicly-funded projects, racist assumptions often blocked the way for African American architects. An example in the early 1970s was the Black American Museum and Cultural Center in Niagara Falls, NY. Coles envisioned the museum, proposed for the heart of the new Rainbow Center project, as portraying Black history and culture in a way that "there will be a demonstrable attitudinal change experienced by those who visit the Museum."

Coles' memory of the presentation about the project in the Niagara Falls City Council chamber is not a happy one. The organization working on the project, according to the project director, activist Frank Mesiah, had requested the city to grant them a two year option to buy a parcel of land for the museum. As Coles and Mesiah recall it, at the end of the presentation, Niagara Falls Mayor, E. Dent Lackey, stated that "black is not a color in the rainbow," and the plan was blocked.

Coles' determination to combat the problems created for African American architects by funding cuts and racism led him to accept a position that brought still more changes for the firm. In 1974 he took a two year sabbatical to join the American Institute of Architects in Washington, DC as Deputy Vice President for Minority Affairs. Coles has said that the move changed his perspective on architecture. The experience completed the transformation that made him a full-time advocate rather than architect by day, activist by night.

The AIA created the position as part of its response to Whitney Young's criticism. A Coles ally was Robert Wilson, an influential Black architect, whom Coles first met in the 1960s. Wilson was one of a group of Black architects in New York City who formed the New York Coalition of Black Architects, with the aim of helping Black architects gain access to major building projects. One early effort was to pressure AT&T to appoint a team of African American architects as associates to Philip Johnson on a major construction project in Manhattan, an effort in which Coles was teamed with Wilson and two others. In 1974, while serving as president of the Connecticut Society of Architects and AIA vice-president, Wilson worked with Coles to develop new initiatives that would assist African American architects.

One goal was to attract more African Americans to the profession.

Drawing of Black American Museum and Cultural Center, Niagara Falls, NY, as envisioned by Coles. The museum was never built. Drawing by Ho Kim.

29

The Lindbergh Center MARTA Station, Atlanta, GA, 1983. See project description, Appendix C, page 73. Photo: Robert T. Coles

That has also been Coles' lifelong aim. It seemed to be a perfect fit of individual passion and institutional goals. However, Coles was frustrated by AIA conservatism. When he proposed that the AIA adopt an affirmative action program to advance women and minorities at its headquarters, he found AIA executive vice president William Slayton's comment, "Coles, your job is not to shake things up around here, it's to make things run smoothly," especially rankling. That just was never Coles' style.

Moreover, given the crisis facing African American architects and their opportunities for getting work, he adopted the stance that his most important task was to help existing Black firms survive. Attracting new Blacks to the profession was, in the short-term, a lower priority. Three of the five goals for 1975 that Coles outlined for the AIA related to professional development among minority architects already in practice, and minority/majority collaborations.

Coles, with assistance from Robert Wilson, organized a one day conference on joint ventures in the spring of 1975, co-sponsored by the AIA and NOMA, to further professional development goals. He had embraced the concept of joint ventures of minority and majority architectural firms as a way to free minority practitioners from simply doing inner city projects. Without the opportunity to design buildings in "prominent public areas," Coles reasoned, minority architects would never receive recognition for work that would lead to significant commissions of their own. The only feasible way to get opportunities to work on prominent projects with substantial budgets, in Coles view, was for small, minority firms to partner with some of the majority-owned giants in the field. The conference brought together some 100 representatives from minority and majority firms to explore ways to formalize joint ventures that equitably divided workloads, responsibilities, and financial obligations to best use the expertise of participating partners to serve clients.

The joint venture concept served Coles' own firm well. In 1980, the firm of Perry, Dean, Stahl, Rogers, successor to Perry, Shaw, Hepburn and Dean, approached its former intern to join its team for the Providence Railroad Station, led by Skidmore, Owings and Merrill. Other participants in the joint venture were consulting engineers Ammann & Whitney of New York. During the project Ammann & Whitney asked Coles to help them win the commission for the $10 million Lindbergh Center MARTA Station in suburban Atlanta. Coles' firm eventually provided architectural services as a consultant for that project, which, in turn, led to Ammann & Whitney's participation as engineers with Coles on the Health, Physical Education and Recreation Complex at SUNY Buffalo. By 1980 a number of major joint ventures were underway, and Coles' firm moved from his home to offices in the historic Ellicott Square Building in downtown Buffalo. Having completed her MBA, Sylvia assumed a new title as Controller/Business Manager to oversee all of the firm's financial activities.

In 1984 Coles was appointed to the New York State Board of Architecture, and used his monthly visits to New York City to market his firm. That resulted in an opportunity to partner with Edward Durrell Stone on building the new College of Staten Island. While he described his role in the Staten Island project

Above and below: Frank Reeves Center for Municipal Affairs, Washington, DC, 1986. See project description, Appendix C, page 78. Photos: Maxwell MacKenzie.

as "very minor," he hired a Director of Operations to run the work and to identify new projects in New York. He eventually collaborated with URS on the $25 million ambulatory care pavilion at Harlem Hospital, and as architect of record on PS 233 in Brooklyn.

While he was working at the AIA, Coles re-established contact with his University of Minnesota schoolmate, Randy Vosbeck. The pair began to put in practice some of the principles of joint venturing that Coles advocated. Specifically, they began to market work in Washington, DC and Buffalo, leading to the design of the $10,000,000 Utica Street Subway station in Buffalo, completed in 1984, and the $35 million Frank Reeves Center for Municipal Affairs in Washington, completed in 1986. To advance the Frank Reeves Center project, Coles and Vosbeck formed a joint venture that included Coles firm, Vosbeck's Washington firm, VVKR, and Devrouax and Purnell, an African American firm based in Washington. Coles opened a branch office in Washington, DC to oversee the Reeves Center project.

Kathryn Prigmore (then Tyler), a young Black architect, was one of five who staffed Coles' Washington branch office. She went on to become an award-winning architect, now with over thirty years in practice. She also served as associate dean/associate professor at Howard University from 1989 to 2003. She served on the Virginia Commonwealth Board for Architects and Engineers, which she chaired from 2000 to 2002. In 2002 she was elevated to the AIA College of Fellows for her contributions to the profession as "an educator, administrator, and state board member," the fifth African American woman out of 2,568 Fellows. She is one of the mentees of whom Coles is so proud, and they remained in contact through the years.

A staff of 12 in Buffalo and five in Washington advanced several major projects in the next few years, all in association with other firms. The Lindbergh Center MARTA Station was completed in 1983. Also in 1983, in association with Corddry, Carpenter, Dietz and Zack, Coles completed the Operations Control Center and South Park Yards and Shops projects for the Niagara Frontier Transportation Authority in Buffalo. The $37 million Providence, Rhode Island Railroad Station was completed the next year. The $27 million Health, Physical Education and Recreation Complex at SUNY Buffalo Amherst Campus was finally constructed in two phases, the second as a joint venture.

The first phase was a 13,000 seat field house, completed in association with Sargent, Webster, Crenshaw and Folley of Syracuse as consulting engineers in 1983. The second phase was an Olympic natatorium, completed as a joint venture with Ammann & Whitney in 1987. The project held major significance for Coles. He was the architect of record this time. To Coles, the complex signified the success of the joint venture plan not only in moving Black architects into the mainstream, but also in moving them from junior partners to initiators of projects.

It was in the midst of all of this design and construction activity in Buffalo and beyond that Coles helped bring the Preservation League of New York's annual meeting to Buffalo in 1980, and Coles took the opportunity to remind Buffalonians that if the city were to thrive, its neighborhoods must thrive, too.

According to the Whitney Young Award nomination for Richard Prosser, it was under Prosser's tutelage that Coles took an active role in the Preservation League, and put into practice some of the concepts he had outlined in "An Architect Looks at Buffalo." He became a trustee of the League,

Utica Street Subway Station, completed in 1984.   Photo: Sylvia Coles

Above: Alumni Arena, Phase I, Health, Physical Education & Recreation Complex at SUNY Buffalo, designed by Coles firm and completed in 1983. Photo: Public Domain

Right: Olympic natatorium, completed as Phase II in 1987. Photo: David Gordon

See project descriptions for each phase, Appendix C, pages 74-75.

and was in his second term when the League chose Buffalo for its 1980 annual conference.

He encouraged the public to attend the conference, "Preservation in the Post-Industrial City: The Value of Neighborhood Conservation." Expressing his passion for the civilizing nature of urban life, and looking at the city holistically, Coles told *Buffalo Evening News* columnist, Karen Brady, "I see this as a very important meeting for Buffalo and the League. The city is typical, is representative of many other middle-sized urban areas in New York State. It has the same pluses, the same minuses, most importantly, the same problems." He noted that "Buffalo is experiencing a major re-awakening to its historic past," and that the wooden housing stock, much of it built between 1880 and 1910, needed significant preservation. "The

Chapter 4: The Firm: New Challenges, New Directions   33

William-Emslie YMCA, Buffalo NY, completed in 1982. Upper and lower level plans below. See project description, Appendix C, page 71. Photo: David Gordon

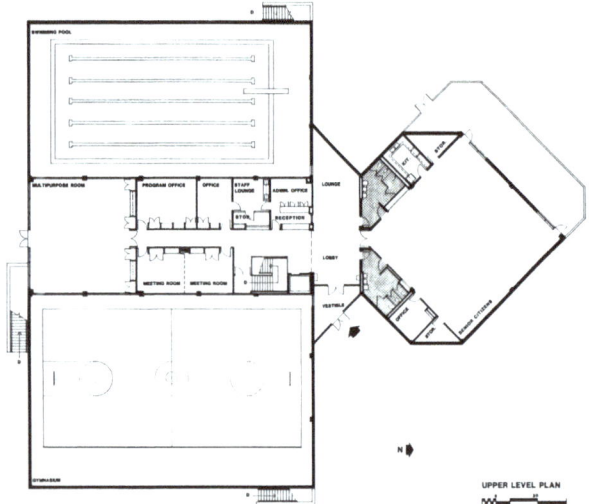

William-Emslie upper level plan

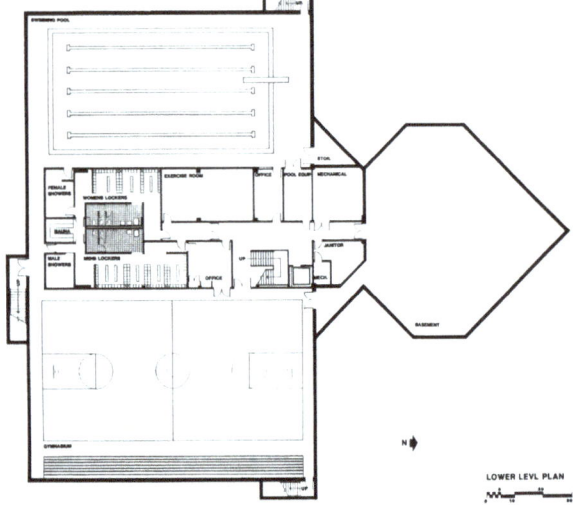

William-Emslie lower level plan

focus of public agencies is Downtown renewal—while the focus should be both Downtown AND neighborhood preservation," he observed. "We shouldn't be living a dichotomy that sees us tearing down substantial buildings downtown while doing very little about the neighborhoods." Brady captured Coles' optimism for the future and enthusiasm about his practice, concluding that Coles "is right here in the city helping not only to create the new but to preserve the old and is thereby making Buffalo better—and more interesting—for all of us."

Nevertheless, despite having contracts for major public buildings and a number of smaller projects, including the William-Emslie YMCA (completed 1982), irregular payments from clients caused cash flow problems that plagued the firm throughout the early 1980s. Sylvia's financial skills helped the firm weather various crises, but as the large projects wound down, new problems arose. By October 1985 the Buffalo staff was reduced to eight, and after completion of the Frank Reeves Center, the Washington office was closed. Sylvia's role changed once again, as she left the firm at the end of 1984, to return later in 1985 as an independent consultant.

Although the Washington office closed, Coles regularly visited the Frank Reeves Center in later years to see how the building and its neighborhood fared. He was well pleased. In 2005 he told colleagues that the building had stood up well to the passage of time. Moreover, it had fulfilled the original vision that planners had for the project, to stimulate additional private development in a blighted area.

Fortunately for the firm, another joint venture, this time with the

Cleveland firm of Voinovich-Sgro, Architects was confirmed in the late 1980s. This project, for the New York State Department of Correctional Services at its Wende Correctional Facility complex in Alden, NY, was to remodel a former county penitentiary into a 700 cell maximum security prison. It included the addition of three major new buildings. The $21.5 million project was completed in 1990.

Other projects completed between 1985 and 1992 included the Bidwell Station Post Office in Buffalo, the Gowanda State Psychiatric Center's Rehabilitation Treatment Center in Gowanda, NY, (both completed 1987), the Ontario County Human Services Office Building in Canandaigua, NY (completed 1990), and the College of Staten Island Conversion (completed 1992). These projects gave the firm new life.

By that time, financial necessity, coupled with Coles passion for educating more minorities to become architects, encouraged him to accept a tenure track faculty appointment at Carnegie Mellon University. The arrangement meant that he spent four days a week in Pittsburgh, and a day a week in either Buffalo or New York administering various commissions.

While joint venturing allowed the Coles firm to survive, the concept was not universally accepted by Black architects, who complained of getting second echelon jobs in white firms, or being relegated to lesser roles in the ventures. One Black principal in his own firm observed that affirmative action laws guaranteed him some work, "but we still get the least." Moreover, "I still do the garbage work." Another concurred, saying, "a white firm feels its role is design, and yours is production. You can't be Black and talented and creative." Others objected that

Bidwell Station Post Office, Buffalo, NY, completed in 1987. Photo: Sylvia Coles

Federal programs involved too much paperwork, and that set-asides only increased tokenism. Nevertheless, Coles felt vindicated by his success with so many joint ventures.

Another concern about joint ventures, affirmative action, and minority set-asides was identified at an AIA/NOMA conference. "The overriding fact of the matter," wrote one participant, "is that there are too few minorities to spread around the country to satisfy state or city objectives in affirmative action." To redress the shortage of trained minority professionals, Coles took on an expanded role in higher education to recruit and train a new generation of minority and women architects.

Gowanda Psychiatric Center Rehabilitation Treatment Center, Gowanda, NY, completed in 1986. Photo: David Gordon

Robert Traynham Coles, FAIA, with Lenore Bethel at the Buffalo & Erie County Historical Society, which hosted an exhibition of Coles' work in 2002. Bethel, a teacher at Locust Street Neighborhood Art Classes, curated the exhibit for El Museo Gallery, and was instrumental in arranging the collaboration between El Museo and the historical society.   Photo: Sylvia Coles

Chapter 5:
Educator and Advocate, . . .
and Service to the Profession

Robert Coles has always been an educator. His formal role in training young architects began after he met Charles Kahn at the 1968 AIA convention. Kahn, the new Dean of the University of Kansas School of Architecture, invited Coles to be a critic for student work, a task he pursued intermittently for twenty years. In 1989 he accepted a position as Langston Hughes Distinguished Professor of Architecture and Urban Design at Kansas. The university had established the chair in 1968 in response to the assassination of Dr. Martin Luther King, Jr., and named it after Hughes, a native son of Lawrence, Kansas. The post required Coles to be in residence for one week a month from January through May.

Appalled by the decline in minority enrollments in schools of architecture at Kansas and across the country, Coles used the occasion of his inaugural lecture to speak about "The Practice of Architecture in a Post-Industrial City: The Profile of a Black Architect—An Endangered Species." Later excerpted as a guest editorial in *Progressive Architecture* as "Black Architects: An Endangered Species," [reprinted in Appendix E, pages 101-102] the talk put Coles at the forefront of an ongoing advocacy campaign to expand the number of minority students in schools of architecture, and to retain them in the profession after graduation.

In his lecture, Coles observed that in the previous two decades the number of architects in the United States approximately doubled. At best, the number of Black architects barely kept pace, remaining at about 2% of the total. In the meantime, between the late 1970s and late 1980s the number of Blacks enrolled in schools of architecture fell from 10% to 5%. Further endangerment, Coles argued, came from Black practitioners being

cut off from the mainstream of the society that controls building resources. ... Those who are in practice focus on public works because of the lack of access to private resources. As public construction shrinks, as affirmative action programs are struck down, as black political power diminishes in our urban centers, black architects are increasingly threatened.

The crisis threatens the profession, which in order to survive must begin to look like the society it must serve—a society which is becoming increasingly minority. It threatens our nation as well, for we can ill afford not to maximize the human resources that we have. We need the best and the brightest to compete, regardless of race.

The AIA responded to Coles' editorial by establishing a task force that confirmed his conclusions in a report released in March 1990. In addition, Coles' editorial caught the attention of Bradford C. Grant, who was teaching architecture at a number of California institutions, and Dennis Alan Mann, who was teaching architecture at the University of Cincinnati. It inspired their further investigation. Grant and Mann included the names of 877 architects in their *Directory of African American Registered Architects*, published in 1991. The study received an AIA honor award. They estimated that 95% of eligible practitioners had been identified and included. This painted an even more dire picture than Coles had, as their number of Black practitioners was about half of Coles' earlier estimate.

The problem was identified, and awareness was increasing. Solutions, though, were more elusive. Coles believed that part of the solution lay in education. Shortly after the "Endangered Species" editorial appeared, Coles accepted the position at Carnegie Mellon beginning in September 1990. Work at his firm had fallen off, and staff had been reduced to one architect, one intern architect, and one administrative assistant. In addition, one architect in New York was supervising work on the Harlem Hospital project. Ever optimistic, Coles saw the Carnegie Mellon appointment as an opportunity to recruit, train and inspire young African American architects.

Central to this effort was the Phelps-Stokes Fund initiative to encourage African American architects to become teachers so that they could, as examples, attract students into schools. "I serve as a marquee," he told a College of Fellows gathering in 1992, "to attract African American students." The Phelps-Stokes Fund initiative's goal was to create more such "marquees" through a collaboration among universities, the AIA College of Fellows, and the Fund. In 1990 the College of Fellows appointed a three member task force to address the problem of declining enrollment of African American students in schools of architecture. The task force was comprised of Coles' friend and Chancellor of the College of Fellows, Robert B. Marquis, former Chancellor William A. Rose, Jr., and Coles. Rose explained his concerns about the underrepresentation of African Americans in the profession to Dr. Wilbert J. Le Melle, President of the Phelps-Stokes Fund. As a former Ford Foundation program director, US Ambassador to Kenya, and President of Mercy College, Le Melle had extensive experience in leadership development and higher education. He suggested that

the most rewarding approach would be to focus on encouraging and supporting more minorities to prepare for academic careers in the under-represented professions such as architecture. The development of a steady flow of professors, with the support of the deans of the schools of architecture, would have the effect of creating a leadership groups of faculty members who would be committed to doing something about this problem. Apart from increasing the number of blacks in the teaching ranks and serving as role models, these professors could have a more than passing impact upon increasing the numbers of minorities in the profession of architecture.

Le Melle, Rose, and Coles subsequently constructed a pilot program to test the concept. Under the plan, the Phelps-Stokes Fund committed itself to a three-year fund drive to raise $5 million to endow programs to attract African American students into various fields of higher education, including $400,000 to attract African American architecture educators. Under the plan, Le Melle expected universities to provide tuition wavers to students as well as teaching assistantships. Foundations and corporations would contribute funds to the endowment, and the Phelps-Stokes Fund would write grant applications, administer funds, and provide mentoring and other support for students. The College of Fellows pledged $5,000 per year for three years if Phelps-Stokes raised the remainder of the $400,000.

The goal was to pair Hampton University with Carnegie Mellon, and Howard University with the University of California at Berkeley to encourage architecture graduates of the Historically Black Universities to pursue post-graduate work. It produced a short-lived collaboration between Carnegie Mellon and Hampton that gave Hampton graduate students the opportunity to continue studies toward master's and doctoral degrees in architecture.

Sadly, after encouraging early reports, the program foundered over institutional misunderstandings about finances, a dearth of corporate funding, and the fact that students found it more attractive to reenter the profession after receiving master's degrees rather than continuing with doctoral work and entering teaching.

Other frustrations, including student apathy, discouraged Coles. To celebrate both Black History Month and Women's History Month in 1992, Coles had invited the Harlem architect, Roberta Washington, with whom he had collaborated on several projects in New York City, and one of the eight women featured in Jack Travis' recently published *African American Architects in Current Practice*, to give a guest lecture. While he was pleased with the lecture, with the fact that Washington received a standing ovation at its end, and that one of the African American students in attendance commented that she was the first lecturer he had heard who addressed "the real issues that architects will face today," Coles was bitterly disappointed at the low student turnout. The ten Black students at Carnegie Mellon had agreed to host a reception prior to the lecture, but only two attended, joined by just three more of their colleagues for the lecture. It was especially disappointing, since Coles had arranged for a large construction company to sponsor the event, and hoped that it would provide students with an important networking opportunity.

"An African Evening", May 1992. Dr. Wilbert Le Melle, center, and Sylvia & Robert Coles on right, with other guests on left.   Photo: Paul Knowles

In addition to student apathy, Coles was disappointed by the lack of support from the administration. Moreover, he felt isolated from the rest of the faculty, especially after the department head, John Eberhard, asked him during a meeting whether he should call him "boy or son." He finally resigned the Carnegie Mellon position in 1995. Nevertheless, he continued to affirm his vision for the profession, both within the academy and within the AIA.

Shortly after leaving Carnegie Mellon, Coles accepted an invitation from the University of South Florida to deliver the Sam Gibbons Eminent Scholars Chair Lecture, a talk about urban waterfronts, at the Tampa Museum of Art [re-printed in Appendix E, pp 103-105]. Well aware that African American practitioners had often been cut out of the country club or other social networks through which white architects learn of projects, Coles used the opportunity to discuss strategies for getting jobs. Drawing on his own experiences, he identified thesis projects, community involvement, various networking opportunities, and developing one's own projects as a client as paths to future commissions.

The vexations of the Carnegie Mellon experience notwithstanding, Coles remained an aggressive advocate for the admission of African Americans into the architectural profession, and their retention. "My great concern and fervent goal," he wrote the AIA in 2002, "is to make this profession look more like the society it has to serve. Of particular concern to me [are] the African-American architects who number no more than 1,500 out of over 100,000 registered architects, or no more than 1.5 percent."

Roberta Washington, elevated to Fellow at the 2006 AIA Convention, with Norma Sklarek, FAIA, to her right. Sklarek was the first African American woman to be elected to the College of Fellows. Photographer unidentified

In 2003 Coles urged that a committee on African American Entrance into the Western New York Architectural Profession be convened, to consist of architectural practitioners and academics, and construction managers. The committee met in the fall of 2003 and winter of 2004 to discuss strategies for attracting and retaining African Americans in the local architectural profession. Coles proposed several strategies that had succeeded in other cities. He hoped to take advantage of a massive Joint Schools Construction Board building program. The mandate to meet minority set-aside requirements, he thought, would provide incentives to educators, majority architectural firms, and contractors to reach out to African American students at a young age.

The committee proposed that the Buffalo Public Schools, Erie Community College, and The State University at Buffalo collaborate to realize that goal. His own alma mater, Technical High School, he wrote, should upgrade its architectural design curriculum into a five-year cooperative program with the Community College. The new program, suggested by Associate Superintendent of Schools, Mel Alston, a former Coles intern, would award graduates both a high school diploma and an associate's degree. To facilitate that plan, Coles also proposed that the Community College offer its Construction Technology and Architectural Technology courses at its city campus as well as at its suburban campuses. Coles saw these changes as creating a feeder for the University's School of Architecture and Planning, and he joined Architecture Chairman, Kent Kleinman, to propose that the University consider offering six

Robert Traynham Coles, FAIA, becomes Chancellor of the College of Fellows, 1994. Photo: Sylvia Coles

or eight week summer workshops in architecture to encourage young people to enter the feeder program and continue their architectural education beyond the community college level. As of this writing, the proposal for a high school architectural program and the summer workshops have not been implemented.

Coles has always seen the University at Buffalo's School of Architecture and Planning, founded in 1969, as a primary vehicle for attracting minorities to the profession, but has been disappointed in its performance in that area., He wrote the chair of the UB architecture department in 2006, that UB had, "a dismal record of African American admissions." Repeating his mantra, that "this profession must look like the society that it has to serve, or it will not survive," Coles reiterated that "the only public school of architecture in New York State . . . can help make that a reality."

He renewed his call for cooperation among the public schools, community college, and university in 2010 to increase the number of minorities in the profession. In April, having been named by local developer L.P. Ciminelli, program manager for the Buffalo school reconstruction program, to develop a plan to increase the number of African American architects in the region, Coles made a presentation to the AIA Buffalo/WNY Chapter board of directors. He called for an overall improvement in the quality of primary education in the Buffalo public schools. He was pleased that the new superintendent of schools hoped to establish architecture programs at Grover Cleveland and Lafayette High Schools, and encouraged him to look at the program already in existence at the Charter High School of Architecture and Design (CHAD) in Philadelphia as an example.

However, he was still unhappy with the university's performance. Despite talks having been held since 2004, he claimed, graduates of the community college's programs were still not admitted freely to the university's school of architecture. He noted that Professors Dennis Mann and Bradford Grant's study of African American architects in the United States showed that the University at Buffalo's program had registered very few African American graduates since 1969 and had no African American faculty members in architecture.

Coles proposed that UB initiate a plan similar to the Phelps-Stokes Fund initiative at Carnegie Mellon. He noted that a recent requirement for registration would make the Master of Architecture degree the first professional degree, and that the requirement would put a considerable financial burden on students in Historically Black Colleges and Universities, and, indeed, on the institutions themselves. He urged the UB department to approach schools of architecture at the Historically Black Colleges and Universities with offers of "ample financial resources" to give their architecture graduates the opportunity to earn their master's degrees at Buffalo. Five years later, though, when Coles wrote the new chairman of the State University Board of Trustees, H. Carl McCall, his frustration that there were no African American faculty in the architecture department, and only ten students in a student body of 300, was palpable.

In 1981, Coles had been elected to the AIA's College of Fellows. His election to the College's Executive Committee in 1991 gave him additional opportunities for advocacy outside of academe. Speaking at the Fellows breakfast at the New York State Association of Architects convention in Newport, Rhode Island in October 1992, Coles, the newly-elected Secretary of the College, cited the leadership role that the College had already taken in diversifying the profession. He went on to urge other Fellows at the breakfast to contribute to the College of Fellows Fund in its effort to raise money to support the Phelps-Stokes initiative, and to become actively involved in promoting diversity. "We need you to stay active, and provide that leadership and assist the Executive Committee in this effort," he admonished attendees. "Get involved—activity and commitment will keep you alive and healthy."

The year after the 1992 Los Angeles riots, with the support of his long-time friend, Randy Vosbeck, Coles was elected Vice Chancellor/Chancellor Elect of the College of Fellows. Coles aspired to use his office to further his advocacy agenda. In July 1993 he circulated a memorandum titled "A Different Urban Agenda for the AIA College of Fellows" to colleagues in the College. In the memorandum he announced his intention to dedicate his tenure as Chancellor to promoting an urban agenda. "My concern," he wrote, "is that the inner cities of our nation are becoming more and more isolated, and that the population—increasingly black, brown and, now yellow—are becoming more estranged from the mainstream of society." The problems that prompted riots in Los Angeles, Atlanta, and Miami must be confronted and solved, he warned, "if we are to survive as a nation." He urged architects to rethink their tendency to seek solutions to urban problems in massive infrastructure and building projects. Instead, he asked them to find ways "to rebuild the human spirit" through small, individual initiatives. "The sum of [those individual] activities," he argued, "can be a major collective effort," but would be more effective than failed, massive initiatives of the recent past. He cited a number of specific examples. One Fellow annually devoted two weeks of his vacation to working with Habitat for Humanity. Another encouraged minority high school students to visit his office so he could show them what minority professionals can do. Such small initiatives would begin "to break down the barriers that separate the haves from the have-nots in our country."

His elevation to Chancellor in December 1994, the highest position an architect can achieve in the College of Fellows, was the apex of his career but not yet the culmination of his efforts, which continued throughout the years. He received little support for the urban initiative, but did induce Harvey Gantt, FAIA, the former mayor of Charlotte, North Carolina, to give the keynote address at the College of Fellows Convocation banquet during the AIA annual convention in Atlanta. Moreover, Dr. Sharon Sutton, FAIA, professor of architecture at the University of Washington, agreed to give the invocation. Coles chose the pair because both were "committed advocates," and

Celebrating Coles' election to Chancellor of the AIA College of Fellows are R. Randall Vosbeck, center, and Kathryn Prigmore, Dec. 1994. Photo: Sylvia Coles

Johnnie B. Wiley Pavilion, a re-purposing of Buffalo's War Memorial Stadium
Photo: William H. Siener

neither disappointed him. Sutton, he wrote later, "emotionally moved the attendees," who gave her a standing ovation. Gantt challenged the audience "in a speech as powerful as Whitney Young's."

Still, he remained frustrated by what he saw as the AIA's limited interest in recruiting and retaining minorities. In 1999 he attended a reception honoring the new AIA president held at the French Embassy in Washington, DC. Afterwards he reflected, "I took note that out of the 500 or more people there, I was the only African American Architect present. Yes, there were African American staff members, African American waiters, and even an African American member of the string quartet. I have told this organization of over sixty thousand members and its leadership that they must do more to make the organization look more like the society that it serves—I wonder when they'll begin the effort. A Diversity conference once a year is not the answer."

Commuting between Pittsburgh and Buffalo, serving in high office in the AIA while teaching full time and administering several projects took its toll, however. In March 1995 he resigned as Chancellor to devote more attention to the practice. The firm completed a number of small commissions in the mid-1990s.

An especially interesting project for Buffalonians was the Johnnie B. Wiley Pavilion. The project re-purposed the site of the old War Memorial Stadium, the original home of the Buffalo Bills, as a community athletic complex also used by east side public schools. The imposing entrance to the old stadium has been preserved in the design. The athletic complex was completed in 1993, and Pavilion offices in 2001. Coles also completed the Hamlin Park Historic Preservation Study in Buffalo in 1998. These projects were followed by two major projects in New York, the expansion and modernization of Public School 233 in Brooklyn, and a new ambulatory care facility for the Harlem Hospital Center (both completed 1998). A project to replace 30,000 seats in Ralph Wilson Stadium, home of the Buffalo Bills (completed 1999), rounded out the 1990s.

Coles' civic activism continued into the new century. He remained an activist even in his recreational pursuits. Soon after arriving in Buffalo, he had turned to sailing as a relief from the pressures of his prac-

Public School 233, Brooklyn, NY, completed in 1998.   Photo: Zbig Jedrus

tice and from May through October every summer he sailed his own boat from the Small Boat Harbor on the Buffalo waterfront into Lake Erie. He bought a 16 foot Snipe in 1963 in which he learned to sail, later replacing it with a 22 foot boat in 1969, and the 25 foot *Moorjoy* in 1978. Even his love of sailing connected with his thoughts about the city. In an *Artvoice* newspaper article titled "Lake Erie is the Best of Buffalo" Coles commented in 2000 that on his boat is "where I dream about what the city can be." With his wife and son, he had also sailed the American and British Virgin Islands and the Abacos, islands in the Bahamas, in chartered sailboats, in the early seventies. To George Arthur, a former Buffalo Common Council President and friend, Coles was the perfect choice to be involved in an event sponsored by the Buffalo & Erie County Historical Society.

The society had contracted with Amistad America, Inc. to bring the freedom schooner *Amistad* to Buffalo in September 2003 as part of the vessel's tour of the Great Lakes. A replica of the ship on which kidnapped West Africans bound for slavery overthrew the captain and crew in 1839, the *Amistad's* mission is to spread the story of the historic incident and to promote improved relationships among races and cultures. George Arthur chaired the Host Committee, which planned a full schedule of activities during the Buffalo visit, including community forums on local issues and receptions at the historical society.

Coles was an active member of the Host Committee, sending letters to the heads of Buffalo's African American organizations, including the NAACP, the Urban League, and the African American Historical Association, inviting them to a gala reception for William Pinkney, then master of the *Amistad*. Coles met Pinkney in April, when he was in Buffalo planning the September visit and found him a "fascinating guy." Larry Paul of the *Buffalo News* described Pinkney as "prominent in his own right . . . the first black man and one of five Americans to solo-circumnavigate the globe by sail around Cape Horn. The author of books and the subject of a PBS special broadcast in 2000, Pinkney lead his crew in telling the tale of this heroic breakout from bondage."

When George Arthur, asked Coles to head the flotilla which would lead the Amistad into the Buffalo Harbor, Coles said, "I didn't hesitate too long to say yes," and invited his long-time sailor friend, Louis Brehm, to sail in with him. On the afternoon of September 10, Coles and Brehm, in *Moorjoy*, with its colorful red, yellow, and orange sail, waited outside the harbor. When the *Amistad* appeared, they led the way, with about seventy-five other boats following. It was a grand moment for Coles. Part of the crowd gathered at the Erie Basin Marina to watch as the *Amistad* and other boats sailed in and the Amistad docked. Coles' wife, Sylvia, and their photographer friend, Hilary Burke, took photographs to record this historic event.

Ronald H. Brown Ambulatory Care Pavilion, Harlem Hospital Center, Harlem, NY, completed 1998. See project description, Appendix C, page 82.
Photo: Zbig Jedrus

Photos above were taken by Sylvia Coles during the historic visit to Buffalo of the freedom schooner ***Amistad***, shown on the right as it sits in the Buffalo Harbor on September 10, 2003. Photo on left is of Captain William Pinkney. The colorful red, yellow, and orange sail seen in the photo in the center identifies Coles' 25 foot sailboat, the ***Moorjoy***.

A dockside reception that evening welcomed Captain Pinkney and his crew, and an interfaith service at St. Paul's Episcopal Cathedral celebrated the legacy and spirit of the *Amistad*. Over the next several days an estimated 25,000 people, including hundreds of school children, visited the ship. Chairman George Arthur, in closing remarks, said the *Amistad's* visit brought a message of reconciliation and harmony among races and promoted unity and a deeper understanding of the cultural diversity in the Buffalo community.

As one who held strong opinions about how decisions in the 1960s and 1970s restricted Buffalo's urban renaissance, Coles was one of the community and economic leaders whom sociologist Diana Dillaway interviewed for her book, *Power Failure*, published in 2006. Coming from a prestigious Buffalo family, Dillaway used her access to the city's most powerful and insightful leaders to reconstruct the factors that led to the city's decline. Based on those interviews, Dillaway concluded that the white business and financial elite, ethnic Catholic neighborhood communities, and the Democratic political machine with its entrenched patronage system, all had vested interests in protecting the status quo. Only the city's African American community promoted an agenda of change, and they were consistently thwarted by a multi-term mayor who diverted community development funds for his own pet projects.

The turn of the new century also saw the completion of several commissions. Among those that sustained Coles' practice until 2012 were the School #38 renovation on Buffalo's West Side (completed 2005); a feasibility study for Public School 118 in the Bronx (completed 2006); the design for a proposed

Jesse Nash, Diana Dillaway, and Robert Coles at a luncheon in 2006.   Photo: Sylvia Coles

Front desk at Merriweather Library. Photo: David Gordon

The "Tile Quilt", a permanent display of ceramic tiles created by the Locust Street Community Art Classes, led by artist Gail McCarthy. See Apollo Theater Project, Appendix C, page 83. Photo: David Gordon

new Public School 128 in Queens (completed 2007); and the Ronald H. Brown Ambulatory Care Facility in Harlem (completed 2012).

The two projects of the period that best reflect Coles' philosophy that architects must "see their architecture as a broad movement to enhance the quality of life of urban people" are located next to each other in the heart of Buffalo's East Side African American community. The Apollo Theater project, completed in 2000, converted an old movie house into the City of Buffalo Media Center and a public access television station. Coles reached out to artist Gail McCarthy and to the Locust Street Community Art Classes, a venerable Buffalo East Side institution offering free art classes to anyone, but especially disadvantaged youth. Locust Street children created ceramic tiles reflecting their lives and aspirations to decorate the lobby, thus making the theater project one that both enhanced and involved the neighborhood. Involving the community has always been something Coles admired and a quality he shared with his friends. In 1995, when he attended the funeral of his friend, Robert Marquis, FAIA, he

The Frank E. Merriweather, Jr. Branch Library, Buffalo, NY. See project description, Appendix C, page 84. Photo: David Gordon

paused as he entered the community center where the service was held and noticed the "playful tile sculpture of animals around the play equipment and sandbox, I could see the deft hand of Bob the designer and how he let the community get involved with this building so they could call it their own."

Next door to the Apollo is the Frank E. Merriweather, Jr. Branch Library that Coles described in 2010 as "his most satisfying project." In many ways the building, though relatively small, reflects the culmination of a 50 year career of architecture and activism. The commission challenged Coles to design a library that in his words, "was functional, yet in its design, became a symbol of the African American traditions of the community and the Library's collections." The building was built to house an important reference collection, a product of community activism.

After Coles consulted with Professor David Hughes of Kent State University, author of *Afro-Centric Architecture* (Greyden Press, 1994), he focused on the African village as a prototype for the library. He chose the dome, triangle, and cylinder, traditional forms in African architecture, to evoke the character of an African village. "The library reading rooms," Coles wrote, "could be considered as homes in the tribal village, with members of the village moving freely between the homes or reading rooms." The library consists of six interconnected circular "houses" hung with murals, and with a sky-lit circulation desk at its heart. Hearkening back to the John F. Kennedy Center concept of his master's thesis, Coles designed the library as a community gathering place, featuring reading rooms, a public access computer lab, a 150 seat auditorium, and an African American Resource room housing the largest collection of African American reference materials in western New York. It embodies Coles' philosophy that in modern urban society, private spaces should become smaller and public spaces should grow to facilitate interaction. The library clearly plays a significant role in civilizing urban space. It is a fitting capstone for Coles' career.

Perhaps it is also fitting that the project, indirectly, gave Coles the opportunity to travel to Africa for his fourth visit. While attending a fund-raiser in Greenwich Village in September 2007, Coles met Deogratias (Deo) Niyizonkiza, a young Burundian temporarily living there. Deo had founded the non-profit Village Health Works, which was working with the Burundian government to establish a new health center in Kigutu, about thirty miles from the capital, Bujumburu. When he saw Coles' photographs and plans of the African-inspired Merriweather Library, he challenged Coles to draw up a 40,000 square foot clinic building along the same lines. Then he invited Coles to accompany him to Kigutu to survey the site.

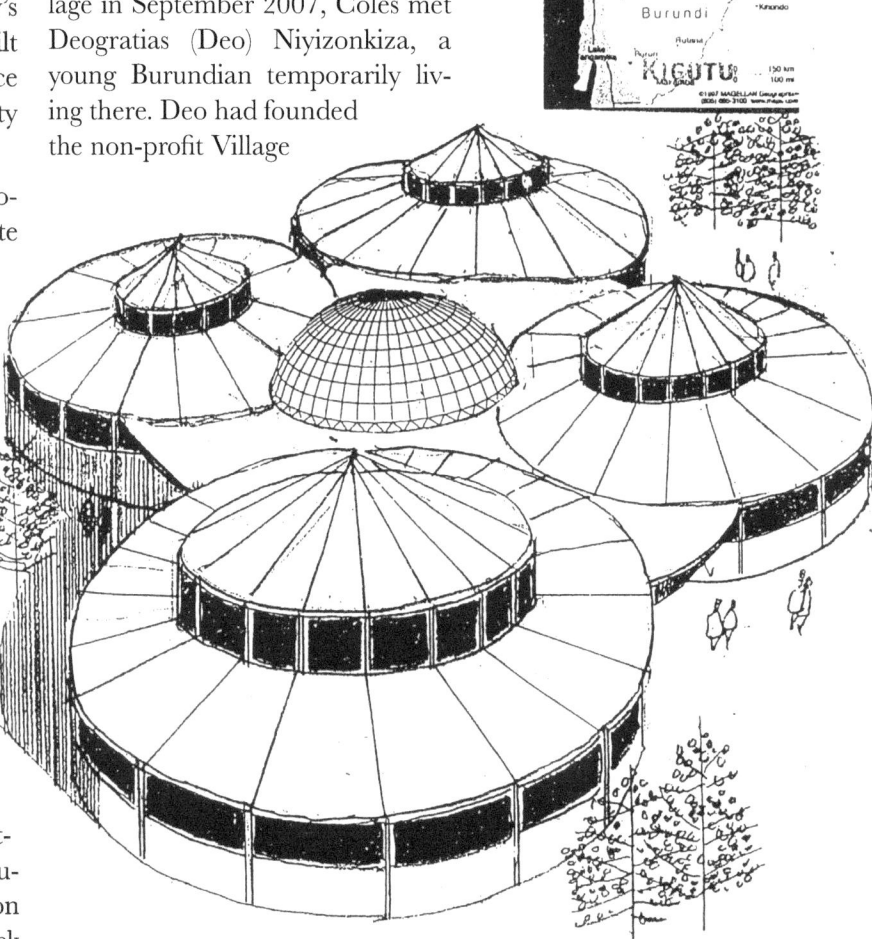

Proposed Kigutu Health Center, Bujumbura, Burundi, 2007
Drawing by Robert T. Coles

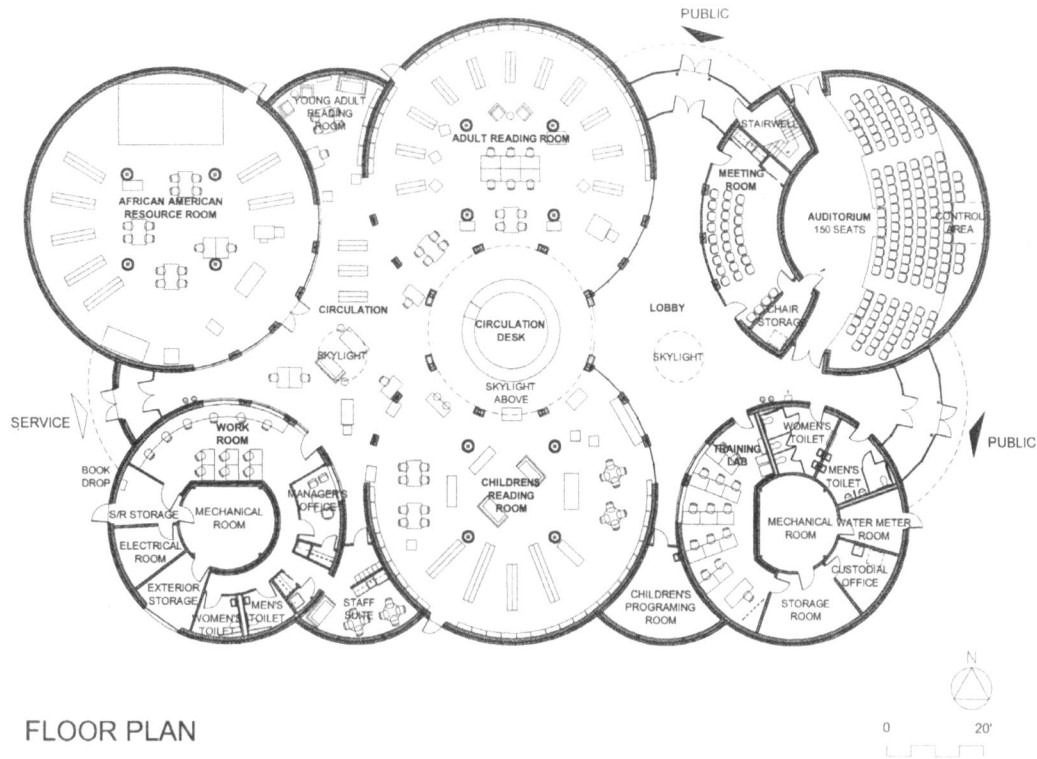

FLOOR PLAN

The design of the Frank E. Merriweather Library (above) inspired the plan for the 40,000 square foot Kigutu Clinic (below). Drawings by Robert T. Coles

Coles spent eighteen days with Deo in Burundi, visiting the site of the proposed new clinic, meeting two physicians and a pre-med student from the US, working in Rwanda and Burundi, and drawing up master plans, the main components of which were a pediatric clinic and a women's clinic. The project, conceived by Burundians, was to be located in a remote area because, Deo told Coles, "That's where the sick people are."

Upon his return to the United States, Coles participated in efforts to raise the funds to build the clinic, attending a fund-raiser in New York, and encouraging friends and acquaintances to contribute. "Deo and his group in Kigutu need help, and they need it now," he wrote in 2008. Coles' vision, as always, was for inspirational architecture to serve as a catalyst to improve peoples' lives. However, the challenges were greater than ever. Once the initial designs were completed, Coles articulated fears that "there will not be enough technical people in Burundi to develop the designs, and there will not be enough money to build the facilities that are so urgently needed." While, in the end, Coles' designs were not utilized for the facilities that were eventually built, he

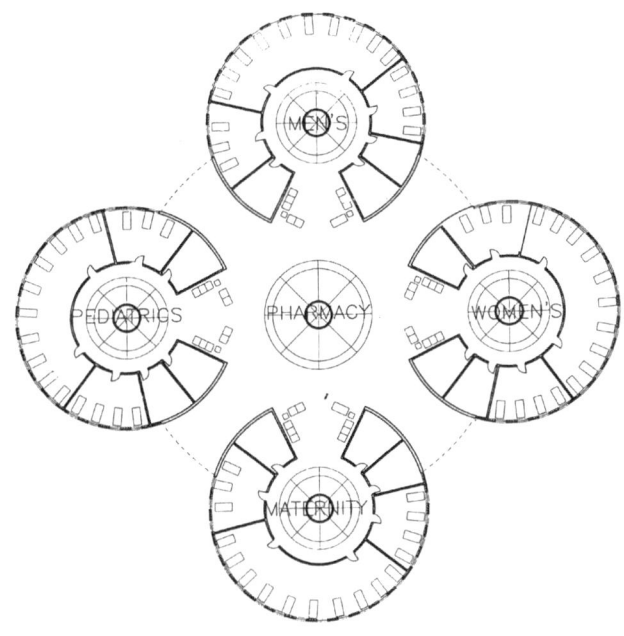

was impressed with the commitment of the people he met. He said, "they know that every person can make a difference, and every person should try."

Chapter 5: Educator and Advocate, and Service to the Profession 47

The James William Kideney
Gold Medal,
AIA New York State, 2004

Chancellor of the AIA
College of Fellows, 1995

Fellow of the
American Institute
of Architects, 1981

Alumni Achievement Award,
University of Minnesota,
College of Architecture &
Landscape Architecture, 1997

Representative of the many honors and awards received by Coles over his long career are the four medals shown above. Photo: L. Kagelmacher

Chapter 6:
Recognition and Unfinished Business

Because of evolving practice changes, Coles decided to close his firm, Robert Traynham Coles, Architect, PC, in December 2012, making it difficult to secure commissions. However, he remains intensely interested in the profession, its diversity, and in the concept of advocacy architecture. Well into his 80s Coles continues to support the ideals of the activist architect that he articulated succinctly in Jack Travis' book, *African American Architects in Current Practice*, published in 1991. Coles wrote:

> *Because they have the ability to see things as they can be, today's architects have a special task which goes beyond simply designing the physical environment. They must be activists involved in the social and political life of the community. They must address their efforts to change in these areas as well, so that people can make the needed adjustments to an increasingly challenging and rich urban world. They must, in their works, build the demonstrative alternative to the way we live today. They must be initiators as well as implementers—leaders more than followers. They must truly be revolutionaries who see their architecture as a broad movement to enhance the quality of life of urban people.*

His designs and advocacy have always been directed toward the goal of enhancing the quality of urban life and enriching the urban world for all who live, or visit, there. He remains frustrated that the vision is not fully realized, and that the growth in the number of African American architects has stagnated. Nevertheless, fellow practitioners, academics, urban planners, and political leaders, both locally and nationally, have admired his work and awarded his efforts on numerous occasions.

By 1968, when the firm was just five years old, Coles had received five awards for design excellence. The first, a First Award, Certificate of Merit for the Sample Memorial Playground at the Chautauqua Institution, Chautauqua, NY, awarded by the AIA Buffalo WNY Chapter in 1967. The New York State Association of Architects cited the same project in 1968. Also in 1968, the firm received an Award of Merit for Excellence in Design, for the Coles residence and studio at 321 Humboldt Parkway from the New York State Association of Architects. The AIA Homes for Better Living Competition recognized Joseph J. Kelly Gardens with an Honorable Mention, and the AIA Buffalo WNY Chapter recognized Friendship House in Lackawanna, NY, with a Design Award the same year. Years later he was still winning awards for excellent design. For example, in 1983, *Progressive Architecture* magazine cited the Providence [Rhode Island] Railroad Station, a joint venture with Skidmore, Owings and Merrill.

Many of his awards for activism note the way that his designs have ameliorated social conditions. For example, Medaille College of Buffalo cited Coles' "professional achievements in interrelating improvements of social and economic conditions with architecture and urban planning" when awarding him the Honorary Doctor of Letters in 1977.

The AIA recognized those same qualities before a national audience in 1981. That year Randy Vosbeck was the AIA president and asked Coles to be his Theme Chairman for the convention, "A Line on Design and Energy," held in Minneapolis. Coles brought together an illustrious group of speakers, including journalist, author, and fellow activist Carl Rowan, whom Coles had met while both were studying at the University of Minnesota. Vosbeck was instrumental in Coles' receiving the Whitney M. Young, Jr. Citation for his contribution to "meeting the architectural profession's responsibility to the social issues of today." His firm, the citation explained, "has served as an example to young blacks in the area and has provided the opportunity for apprenticeship to minority architecture students and graduates." It praised Coles for his contributions to "an architecture of social conscience." He was also named to the AIA College of Fellows.

More awards came in the 1980s and 1990s, including the Buffalo Board of Education's Quality Integration Education Citation in 1989, and Erie Community College's Ebony and Ivory Award in 1993. Again, his achievements in both design and community service were recognized in 1997, when his alma mater, the University of Minnesota College of Architecture and Landscape Archi-

Peter Fleischmann, Board President of the Burchfield Penney Art Center, Robert Coles, Richard Dozier, and David Gordon, photographer, at the Burchfield Penney Exhibition, May 18, 1996. Photo: Sylvia Coles

tecture, presented Coles with the Alumni Achievement Award. The College presents the award annually to an alumna or alumnus "to recognize professional and leadership accomplishments in the design profession." Coles accepted the award and medal at commencement ceremonies in 1997.

Coles' long-time friend, and fellow activist, Dr. Jesse E. Nash, Jr., called his friend "one of Buffalo's finest treasures" at a ceremony recognizing him as Buffalo's Citizen of Distinction in February 1997. Nash recognized and celebrated the inseparability of Coles' architecture, advocacy, and activism. He "took special pains to encourage the development of community entities that creatively used the human capital of the diverse populations that he sought to empower," Nash pointed out. Recognizing what Linda Levine had seen back in 1981, Nash observed that Coles "has not been concerned with simply designing buildings as much as he has demonstrated an interest in constructing cooperative patterns of social interaction . . . ." Challenging the powerful "in the suites for the masses" was not without costs, Nash continued, "what makes Bob so unusual is that time and again he has put his livelihood on the line and paid the price, most frequently in economic terms." Affirming the activism in which he and Coles had long collaborated, Nash urged the mayor and common council to complete the plans for rebuilding the Ellicott District that Coles had begun almost 35 years before. That would be "the real honor for Bob."

In 2004 the New York State Chapter of the AIA recognized Coles with the James William Kideney Award. The award for a lifetime of notable contributions to the profession by an architect is the highest honor granted by AIA NYS.

Coles' work has also been recognized in exhibits at Buffalo's Burchfield Penney Art Center (1996) and at the Buffalo & Erie County Historical Society (2003). The latter exhibit was prepared by Lenore Bethel in conjunction with Buffalo's El Museo Francisco Oller y Diego Rivera, an institution dedicated to producing "exhibitions of contemporary fine art of emerging, mid-career, and

The 2015-2016 *Through These Gates: Buffalo's First African American Architect, John E. Brent* exhibition at the Burchfield Penney Art Center, included an exhibit highlighting Robert Traynham Coles and other architects who followed Brent. This photograph shows a model of the Frank E. Merriweather Library, a photo of the Natatorium at the State University of New York at Buffalo, a photo of the Library's floor plan, two of Coles' many successful projects, and a photo of Coles.

Photo: Tullis Johnson, courtesy of the Burchfield Penney Art Center, 2016

Plaque Dedication for Architect Louise Bethune, October 14, 2012 — Photo: New York State AIA

Left to right: Adriana S. Barbasch, AIA; Dr. Delaine Jones, FAIA; Laura Goodman, AIA; Kelly M. Hayes, AIA; Susan McClymonds, AIA; Barbara Rodriguez, AIA; Kathy Thompson Less, Robert T. Coles, FAIA

established regional, national, and international artists of color". In an introductory essay for the Burchfield Penney exhibit, Dr. Richard K. Dozier, AIA, described Coles as a "local and national trail blazer" who "has built his way to the top of the profession." He continues:

> Coles has unmistakably woven his drive for equality, opportunity, and love and concern into the social and architectural fabric of Buffalo. . . . Importantly, he has done it with sensitivity, care, and commitment few architects could equal. He has infused his local vision of Buffalo with a vitality and creativity that makes a strong statement for the African-American architect in both Western New York and across the country. He has extended his efforts, energies, and effectiveness to the future, affecting architects of tomorrow with his involvement. If the Black architect is in fact moving off the endangered species list, it is due in large part to the efforts of architects such as Robert Traynham Coles.

More recently Coles' work was featured as part of the Burchfield Penney's exhibit "Through These Gates: Buffalo's First African American Architect, John E. Brent," from the fall of 2015 through the spring of 2016.

Award presentations and exhibits have given others the opportunity to express what Robert Coles has meant to them. When AIA Buffalo/WNY presented him the Robert and Louise Bethune Award in 2009, the chapter did just that. Citing his Buffalo East Side home, and the Frank E. Merriweather, Jr. Library as examples of design excellence, the award citation notes also that throughout his career, Coles "has been relentless in his pursuit of addressing the lack of diversity in the profession of architecture." While the Merriweather Library "is a signature building . . . and a beacon for the community," Coles, himself is a beacon and mentor for young architects. "He has been a symbol of an activist architect in Buffalo for almost five decades," the citation concludes.

Coles, though, also took the opportunity to tell the audience what was most important to him about his career. He likened himself to Bethune, the nation's first woman professional architect, in having

Chapter 6: Recognition and Unfinished Business 51

Dr. Sharon E. Sutton, FAIA, accepts the 2011 Whitney M. Young, Jr. Citation at the AIA National Convention in New Orleans. Photo: Oscar & Associates

been discouraged from pursuing a career in a profession dominated by white men. "My firm has designed over 100 buildings," he remarked with pride, but "what I am most proud of are the [nearly] 30 interns—minorities and women—who passed through our office in search of their dreams and who are critical in the design of our very diverse cities of the future."

The New York State AIA recognized Coles' lifetime commitment to mentorship again in 2011 when it awarded him the prestigious Fellows Award. Established in 2006, the award honors "a Fellow of the AIA who has exemplified the philosophy of Mentorship within the profession . . . who has exceeded in helping a young architect, student or an unlicensed individual to gain a greater knowledge of the profession and has assisted them in achieving more than they would have normally within the profession without this guidance."

Richard Dozier's comments notwithstanding, Coles understands that the business of creating a diverse profession to design diverse cities is still unfinished. While still at Carnegie Mellon in the 1990s, Coles had established a working relationship with Dr. Sharon Sutton, professor of architecture at the University of Washington. She was also wrestling with the issues of the Black architect's problem of getting work, and the entrance of African Americans into the profession.

Sutton's 1993 article, "The Progress of Architecture" in *Progressive Architecture*, brought her to Coles' attention. In the article Sutton argued positions very similar to Coles' own. She advocated a role for architects as "agents of change" rather than "powerless actors in a socio-political drama." She asked "are we needlessly succumbing to an outdated image of product-oriented practice? Is it possible to reinvent a field in which we not only design buildings but also seek to mold the public's conception of built environments?" She decried "the commodification of real estate [that] has relegated [architects] to the role of 'servant' for venture capitalists, a role that has proved especially elusive for black architects," given the way in which the profession boomed in the early twentieth century, buoyed by cozy relationships between gentlemen practitioners and their extremely wealthy clients. She called for "a bolder practice of architecture, in which we acquire the intellectual, political, and economic resources to implement social change." This was an activist architect soul mate with whom Coles would forge a collaborative association. Dr. Sutton led a 29 month study for the Ford Foundation, completed in 2006, of Urban Youth Programs in America.

Coles' collaboration with Sutton continued at the 2009 AIA Convention in San Francisco. At a reception there, Coles objected to an AIA diversity initiative on the grounds that it lumped together African American, Asian, Hispanic and white female students to the disadvantage of African Americans, who, he argued, faced different challenges. They more often came from inner cities where educational opportunities were limited, and also lacked economic resources and family support systems necessary for success. He, Sutton, and Randy Vosbeck developed a proposal for the Latrobe Prize, a grant offered by the AIA College of Fellows to fund innovative approaches to architecture and technology.

Sutton submitted the proposal to further study the needs of the most disadvantaged students and how to attract them to architecture. The plan, to begin in 2009, was "to expand traditional disciplinary boundaries and broaden the human resources available to the architecture profession by increasing its attractiveness as a career for African Americans." The proposed project would document the reasons for success at five schools of architecture that had managed to attract, advise, and retain Black students. Sutton was to be the Principal Investigator, assisted by an Advisory Board of ten academics and practitioners, including Bradford Grant and Dennis Mann, authors of the *Directory of African American Registered Architects*, inspired by Coles "endangered species" editorial. Coles and Vosbeck were to coordinate the Advisory Board, and provide feedback on the investigation's findings.

Coles' proposals at the time the Joint Schools Construction Board's revitalization program was announced (see above p. 39), drew, in part, on insights learned from his collaboration with Sutton.

Coles continued to be dissatisfied with UB's efforts to recruit minority students, so when the search for a new Dean for the School of Architecture and Planning (SA+P) opened in 2010, he proposed Sutton for the opening. He reiterated his charge that the school had a dismal record of enrolling African American students even if it had met enrollment goals for women. He went on to point out that of approximately 20 African American students enrolled in the school's history, only six African American graduates had actually been licensed. Sutton, he argued, had the skills to organize a serious recruitment program and to mobilize resources to implement it.

Sutton's candidacy did not succeed, and an internal candidate, Robert G. Shibley, FAIA, was selected as the new Dean in October 2010. Following Shibley's selection, Coles continued to press the school to adopt policies to help diversify the profession. He formed a committee of concerned architects to engage the dean in discussions. As a result, Shibley organized a meeting on Ethnic and Gender Diversity in the Professions of Architecture and Planning and in the School of Architecture and Planning. At the meeting in July 2011, architects and planners and students, faculty and staff from SA+P discussed challenges and opportunities for the University, and strategies to draw a more diverse body of students to the school.

Paul Devrouax, FAIA; Marshall Purnell, FAIA; R. Randall Vosbeck, FAIA; and Robert Traynham Coles FAIA, at Purnell's Inauguration as the 84th and first Black President of the AIA College of Fellows, Dec., 2007.   Photo: Sylvia Coles

As the first decade of the 21st century drew to a close, there was more evidence that the profession nationally was recognizing that issues Coles had raised decades before really need to be resolved. Diversifying the student population at UB and other schools of architecture was only part of the problem. Providing a supportive environment, role models within the faculties and in major firms, and making sure that minority architects have visible roles on a firm's major projects were also concerns that needed attention if minorities were to be recruited to and retained in the profession. In his roles as practitioner, AIA official, educator, mentor and advocate, Coles had been addressing the issues for decades.

Partly through the efforts of Coles and a group of pioneer African American architects, more minorities are rising to positions of leadership and influence in the AIA and in many schools of architecture. In 2007, for example, Marshall Purnell, FAIA, one of Coles' partners on the Frank Reeves Center project that Coles dubbed "the most successful majority/minority joint venture in Washington's history," was elected as the AIA's 84th and first Black President. He and others are making issues of diversity a priority, and even adopting new media to keep those issues in front of the profession. Purnell believes that "fueling the diversity pipeline with fresh faces is architecture's best hope." In May 2009, *Architectural Record* launched a new section of its web site covering diversity in the architectural profession.

In addition to leadership changes at the top of the profession, *Architectural Record* in 2009 pointed to the emerging diversity pipeline as a hopeful development leading to a more diverse profession. The pipeline consists of a number of creative high school programs across the country, like Philadelphia's Charter High School of Architecture and Design, largely populated by minority students who, like Coles, are exposed to the possibilities of architecture as a career. Purnell, like Coles as a practitioner and educator, is acutely aware of his own importance as a role model. He commented, "It wasn't until college that I met my first black architect. I said, 'if he can do this, I can do this.'" He hopes that students he encounters are inspired by his success and receive a message that there ARE opportunities for African Americans in architecture, contrary to what Coles' teacher told him in the 1940s. Some of these recent trends reflect the ideas Coles proposed in his 1993 call for a different urban agenda.

As *Architectural Record* points out, some major public and private commissions awarded to African American-owned firms are hopeful signs that such opportunities are on the rise. One such commission is the National Museum of African American History and Culture, a $500,000,000 project that opened in September 2016 on the National Mall in Washington, DC. An earlier example, the Ohio Environmental Protection Agency headquarters, completed in 1990 by a private developer, was awarded to the nation's largest Black-owned architecture firm, Moody Nolan, partly because its capabilities were at least comparable to majority-owned firms, but also because of its prior experience with public facilities. The former represents a competitive advantage for minority firms. The experience offers an opportunity to transition from public projects and set asides as governments turn more and more to private developers.

Despite these hopeful signs, there are still barriers to overcome. While white institutions are making efforts to recruit more minorities, many observers feel they have not gone far enough to ensure that a supportive environment exists once these students arrive on campus. Steven Lewis, AIA, stated "When you layer the race issue on top of the very cold and competitive studio culture it complicates matters." Others have commented on the lack of role models. Mark Robbins, dean of the Syracuse University School of Architecture reflected that minority students "should be able to find themselves within the faculty," as well as in senior management positions in the field.

A number of informants also lamented to *Architectural Record* about the lack of role models in senior management positions out in the field. Many observers believe lingering racism is keeping minorities down. "The important factor in successfully building a client base and getting ahead is not so much what firm principals say about a person of color but what's said when they're not in the room," observed Dr. Ted Landsmark, then president of Boston Architectural College. "Firms have to provide access to clients. That will enable more people of color to demonstrate the talents they have." Moreover, a number of other business practices need to change in order to recruit and retain more minorities, some professionals told *Architectural Record*. Hiring interns with the intent of keeping them on long-term, would help, some said, as would the AIA's taking leadership in publicizing best practices in recruitment, promotion, and retention.

Coles keeps his eye on the prize of a more diverse profession. For years he has argued for the importance of excellent early education, accomplished role models in faculties and firms, proper financial and intellectual support for minorities in schools of architecture, and greater access for minorities to major projects in public places. Even though the task is not complete, Robert Traynham Coles can be proud of his legacy. The built environment of his home town, and other cities, too, has been enhanced and civilized by his thoughtful creativity. He has begun the process of change in his profession. Most of all, he has inspired younger generations of architects to make a difference in both arenas—architecture and activism.

APPENDIX A

HONORS & AWARDS
1955 - 2016

Robert Traynham Coles, FAIA, receiving the Whitney Young Citation from R. Randall Vosbeck, FAIA, May, 1981.   Photo: Mel Jacobsen

Year Awarded	Awards, Citations	Sponsor
1955	Rotch Traveling Scholarship	Boston Society of Architects
1960	Sterling Forest, N.Y. Residence	Homes for Better Living Award
1965	One of the Nine Best Buildings in Buffalo of all Time, John F. Kennedy Center Buffalo, NY	Buffalo/Western New York Chapter, AIA Buffalo, NY
1968	Award of Merit for "Excellence in Design" Residence and Studio Buffalo, NY	NY State Association of Architects
1968	Joseph J. Kelly Gardens Buffalo, NY	Honorable Mention, AIA Homes for Better Living Competition, Design Award
1968	Friendship House Lackawanna, NY	Buffalo/Western New York Chapter, AIA Buffalo, NY
1967, 1968	First Award, Certificate of Merit, Sample Memorial Playground Chautauqua Institution Chautauqua, NY	Buffalo/Western New York Chapter, AIA, New York State Association of Architects
1977	Honorary Doctor of Letters	Medaille College, Buffalo, NY
1981	Whitney M Young, Jr. Citation	American Institute of Architects
1981	Elevated to Fellow	American Institute of Architects

Year Awarded	Awards, Citations	Sponsor
1986	Design Award, Public Pools Natatorium, SUNY at Buffalo	National Spa and Pool Institute
1989	Quality Integrated Education Citation	Buffalo, NY Board of Education
1993	Ebony and Ivory Award	Erie Community College Buffalo, NY
1997	Alumni Achievement Award	University of Minnesota College of Architecture & Landscape Architecture
1997	Citizen of Distinction	City of Buffalo, NY
2004	James William Kideney Award	New York State AIA, Buffalo, NY
2009	Robert and Louise Bethune Award	Buffalo/Western New York Chapter, AIA, Buffalo, NY
2011	Fellows Award	2011 Honors Awards Jury New York State AIA, Albany, NY
2016	Diversity Award	Buffalo/Western New York Chapter, AIA, Buffalo, NY

Year	Exhibitions	Sponsor
1996	Robert Traynham Coles, Architectural Exhibit	Burchfield Penney Art Center Buffalo, NY
2002	Robert Traynham Coles: Inner City Architect Exhibit	Buffalo & Erie County Historical Museum Buffalo, NY
2015-2016	Through These Gates: Buffalo's First African American Architect, John E. Brent	Burchfield Penney Art Center Buffalo, NY

THE AMERICAN INSTITUTE OF ARCHITECTS

IS HONORED TO CONFER THE

1981 WHITNEY M. YOUNG JR. CITATION

ON

ROBERT TRAYNHAM COLES, FAIA

ARCHITECT, EDUCATOR, COMMUNITY LEADER
AND ACTIVIST IN THE SERVICE OF
THE HIGHER QUALITY OF URBAN LIFE.
THROUGH ADVOCACY AND EXAMPLE,
HE HAS BEEN AN INSPIRATION TO THE YOUNG
AND A CONSCIENCE TO THE ESTABLISHMENT;
THROUGH HIS VISION AND ENTHUSIASM,
HE HAS HELPED REVITALIZE HIS CITY,
AND HAS CONTRIBUTED TO THE CAUSE
OF SOCIAL JUSTICE FOR ALL.

MAY 1981

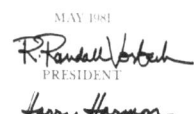

PRESIDENT

SECRETARY

APPENDIX B

PROJECT LISTING
1958 - 2012

Year Completed	Project Name	Cost	
1958	Residence, Sterling Forest, N.Y.	24,500	
1961	Residence for Mr. and Mrs. Robert Coles, Buffalo, N.Y.	--	
1963	John F. Kennedy Recreation Center, Buffalo, N.Y.	1,500,000	X
1964	Lanigan Field House, Buffalo, N.Y.	250,000	
1966	Residence for Mr. and Mrs. Ernst Gehres, Grand Island, N.Y.	--	
1966	Townsend Dental Clinic, Buffalo, New York	--	X
1967	Friendship House of Lackawanna, Lackawanna, N.Y.	550,000	X
1967	Joseph J. Kelly Gardens Housing for the Elderly, Buffalo, N.Y.	750,000	X
1967	Sample Memorial Playground, Chautauqua, N.Y.	25,000	X
1968	Solomon Sculpture Court, Buffalo, N.Y.	--	
1968	Residence for Mr. and Mrs. Gerald Berlyn, Worcester, Mass.	--	
1968	Weekend House for Dr. and Mrs. Joseph Ravin, Orchard Park, N.Y.	--	
1968	Local 34, Inc. – Renovation, Buffalo, N.Y.	300,000	
1969	Weekend House for Drs. Frank Evans and Lydia Wright, Attica, N.Y.	--	
1971	Residence for Mr. and Mrs. Charles Eppolito, Orchard Park, N.Y.	--	
1971	Bacon Hall - Renovation, Buffalo, N.Y.	750,000	
1972	Sherman L. Walker Human Services Center, Buffalo, N.Y.	1,000,000	
1972	Urban Park Housing Development, Rochester, N.Y.	5,500,000	X
1973	Northeast Neighborhood Facility, Rochester, N.Y.	1,000,000	
1973	Ellicott Neighborhood Advisory Council/UDC Housing Project, Buffalo, N.Y.	5,250,000	
1974	Perry Cay Care Center, Buffalo, N.Y.	100,000	
1974	Sperry Playground, Buffalo, N.Y.	100,000	
1975	New Elementary School No. 40, Buffalo, N.Y.	2,100,000	X
1975	Jesse E. Nash, Jr. Health Center, Buffalo, N.Y.	750,000	
1978	Sherman L. Walker Human Services Center – Renovation, Buffalo, N.Y.	225,000	
1978	West Seneca Branch Post Office, West Seneca, N.Y.	750,000	
1979	Federal Office Building – Renovation, Buffalo, N.Y.	200,000	
1980	One Niagara Square – Renovation, Buffalo, N.Y.	100,000	
1981	Rosalia Street Telephone Garage – Renovation, Buffalo, N.Y.	100,000	
1981	VA Medical Center Supply Processing – Renovation, Buffalo, N.Y.	1,895,000	
1981	5 Spaces, VA Medical Center – Renovation, Buffalo, N.Y.	238,000	
1981	Niagara Community Center & Girls Club, Niagara Falls, N.Y.	280,000	
1981	Black American Museum & Cultural Center, Niagara Falls, N.Y.	N/A	
1982	Façade Rehabilitation for Hertel Avenue Stores, Buffalo, N.Y.	160,000	
1982	Jefferson Avenue Façade Signage and Rehabilitation Program, Buffalo, N.Y.	332,000	

Year Completed	Project Name	Cost
1982	William-Emslie YMCA, Buffalo, N.Y.	2,000,000 X
1983	Operations Control Center, Buffalo, N.Y.	2,000,000 X
1983	Lindbergh Center Station, Atlanta, Ga.	10,175,000* X
1983	157 Delaware Avenue – Renovation, Buffalo, N.Y.	77,000
1983	Health, Physical Education & Recreation Complex, Phase I – Alumni Arena, State University of New York at Buffalo, Amherst Campus, Amherst, N.Y.	13,100,000* X
1983	South Park Yards & Shops, Buffalo, N.Y.	10,790,000* X
1984	Providence Railroad Station, Providence, R.I.	37,000,000* X
1984	Removal of Architectural Barriers, Various Resident Engineers Offices, Western N.Y.	250,000
1984	Utica Station, Buffalo, N.Y.	9,683,000* X
1985	Erie Community College City Campus – Teaching Kitchen – Phase I, Buffalo, N.Y.	400,000
1985	Repair & Alteration Program, Buffalo/Western New York Post Offices	N/A
1986	Frank Reeves Municipal Center, Washington, D.C.	35,000,000* X
1986	Buffalo Psychiatric Center – Dining Room Addition, Buffalo, N.Y.	320,000
1987	Bidwell Station Post Office, Buffalo, N.Y.	1,414,000 X
1987	Health, Physical Education & Recreation Complex, Phase II – Natatorium, State University of New York at Buffalo, Amherst Campus, Amherst, N.Y.	12,590,000 X
1988	Asarese-Matters Recreation Center, Buffalo, N.Y.	1,200,000 X
1988	Erie Community College City Campus – Teaching Kitchen, Ph. II, Buffalo, N.Y.	200,000
1989	Research Institute of Alcoholism – Renovation, Buffalo, N.Y.	963,000
1989	Burgard Vocational High School – Addition & Reconstruction, Buffalo, N.Y.	1,438,000
1990	Wende Correctional Facility – Renovation/New Construction, Alden, N.Y.	21,500,000*
1990	Geneva B. Scruggs Health Center Renovation, Women & Children's Unit, Buffalo, N.Y.	193,000
1990	State University College at Brockport Roof Replacement Projects, Brockport, N.Y.	2,900,000
1990	Rehab Treatment Center, Gowanda Psychiatric Center, Gowanda, N.Y.	4,500,000 X
1990	Gethsemane Baptist Church – Addition, Buffalo, N.Y.	500,000
1991	Albion Community Residence, Albion, N.Y.	517,000
1992	Human Services Office Building, County of Ontario, New York, Canandaigua, N.Y.	6,500,000 X
1992	Business Office Building and Campus Demolition, College of Staten Island, N.Y.	2,000,000*

Year Completed	Project Name	Cost
1993	War Memorial Stadium Demolition & Construction of New Athletic Facility, Buffalo, N.Y.	5,500,000
1994	Geneva B. Scruggs Center, 1460 Main Street Renovation, Buffalo, N.Y.	600,000
1994	Geneva B. Scruggs Intermediate Care Facility, Buffalo, N.Y.	450,000
1994	Tauriello-Lakeview Homes, Buffalo, N.Y.	3,047,000
1996	Offices for Watts Engineers, Buffalo, N.Y.	275,000
1997	Conway Field Shelter/Concession Stand, Buffalo, N.Y.	294,000
1998	Hamlin Park Historic Application, Buffalo, N.Y.	N/A
1998	Reconstruction of Westside & Genesee Street Community Centers, Buffalo, N.Y.	265,000
1998	Public School 233 Addition & Modernization, Brooklyn, N.Y.	15,000,000*
1998	Harlem Hospital Center – New Ambulatory Care Facility, New York, N.Y.	25,000,000*
1999	Ralph Wilson Stadium Lower Bowl Seating Replacement, Orchard Park, N.Y.	5,073,000
2000	Langston Hughes Center Renovation, Buffalo, N.Y.	600,000
2000	Renovation of Apollo Theater into a Public Access Television Station, Buffalo, N.Y.	3,414,000 X
2001	JFK Playground Shelter, Buffalo, N.Y.	306,000
2001	Johnnie B. Wiley Pavilion Offices, Buffalo, N.Y.	550,000
2005	School #38 Renovation, Buffalo, N.Y.	6,927,000
2006	Frank E. Merriweather, Jr. Branch Library, Buffalo, N.Y.	4,500,000 X
2006	Program Study, Middle College High School, Buffalo, N.Y.	8,200,000
2006	Public School 118 Feasibility Study, Bronx, N.Y.	N/A*
2007	Public School 128 Design, Queens, N.Y.	45,000,000*
2007	Kigutu Health Center Study, Bujumbura, Burundi	N/A
2012	Dormitory Authority State of New York, Harlem Hospital Center Certificate of Occupancy, Harlem, N.Y.	1,000,000

-- Cost figures not available
N/A Not applicable (project not built)
* Joint Venture project
X Expanded description in Appendix C, Selected Projects

APPENDIX C

SELECTED PROJECTS

John F. Kennedy Recreation Center

Buffalo, New York

Client: City of Buffalo

Architect: Robert Traynham Coles, Architect

Completed: 1963

This multi-purpose recreation complex is located on a 25 acre site in the center of a 160 acre urban renewal project. It was built as a non-cash grant-in-aid by the City of Buffalo. The project consists of a center building of 35,000 square feet housing a gymnasium, multi-purpose meeting room, golden age and health facilities. Lockers serve the building as well as the adjacent 50 meter swimming pool and diving pool. The extensive outdoor athletic areas contain a tot-lot, children's playground, paved game court, baseball, football and soccer fields, and tennis courts. It was cited as one of the nine best buildings in Buffalo of all time by the Buffalo/Western New York Chapter, AIA.

Photo: William H. Siener

Townsend Dental Clinic

Buffalo, New York

Client: Dr. James Townsend
Architect: Robert Traynham Coles, Architect
Completed: 1966

This project is a small clinic with four examination rooms serving the nearby residential community. Located on a small site on a main thoroughfare, it focuses on an adjacent park which provides for a permanent vista and adjacent open space in an otherwise densely developed neighborhood. The strong articulated roof provides clerestory light for the operatories and enhances the vertical scale of the one-story building.

Photo: Gerard Myers

Friendship House

Lackawanna, New York

Client: Friendship House of Lackawanna, Inc.
Architect: Robert Traynham Coles, Architect
Completed: 1967

This 20,000 square foot settlement house (demolished in 2014), clad in exposed weathering steel and glazed brick, was located on a five-acre site in the home of the fourth largest steel mill in the world. The building was decorated with bright and cold colors on the interior to contrast with the dreary exterior environment. All major spaces were grouped around three interior courts; There were no exterior windows.

Award: 1968 Design Award
Buffalo/Western New York Chapter, AIA

Photo: Gerard Myers

Joseph J. Kelly Gardens - Housing for the Elderly
Buffalo, New York

Client: Buffalo Municipal Housing Authority
Architect: Robert Traynham Coles, Architect
Sculpture: Marilyn Stone
Completed: 1967

This 44 unit development is located on a linear urban site adjacent to a detached dwelling neighborhood. The combined one and two story development was designed as an integral part of that neighborhood. The six residential buildings are sited perpendicular to the street. with public and private courts developed between them. Sculptural screens and fountains satisfy both functional and aesthetic needs.

Award: 1968 Honorable Mention
AIA Homes for Better Living Competition

Photo: Gerard Myers

Appendix C: Selected Projects   67

Paul Lindsay Sample Memorial Playground

Chautauqua Institution, Chautauqua, New York

Client: Helen Heinz Sample
Architect: Robert Traynham Coles, Architect
Completed: 1967

Located on a peninsula overlooking Chautauqua Lake, this project served as a living memorial in honor of a former president of the institution. To provide protection from the often strong prevailing winds, a circular mound was developed with a sand-filled recess with four pieces of brightly-painted welded steel play sculpture. A circular ramp around the play area provided a sitting area for mothers as well as spectator seating for nearby sailing events. The plaque appropriately read "To the Children of Chautauqua."

Awards: 1968 Certificate of Merit-Excellence in Design, New York State Association of Architects
1968 Design Award, Buffalo/Western New York Chapter, AIA

Photo: Paul Maze/Phototech

Urban Park Housing Development

Rochester, New York

Client: Catholic Interracial Council
Architect: Robert Traynham Coles, Architect, PC
Completed: 1972

This high density housing medium income project in Rochester's Third Ward Urban Renewal Area included an 11-story high rise building containing 100 units for the elderly, and 154 family units in 14 low rise building on the six acre site. The low rise family units contain two, three and four bedroom units grouped around a series of activity courts. The high rise building contains efficient, one and two family units. Community facilities such as a laundromat and social spaces are located in the high rise building as well as the management office. An exterior cladding of exposed concrete block is used on both the high rise and low rise buildings to unify the development.

Photographer unknown

Appendix C: Selected Projects

New Elementary School No. 40

Buffalo, New York

Client: Board of Education, City of Buffalo
Architect: Robert Traynham Coles, Architect, PC
Completed: 1975

The program called for the development of a K-6 elementary school of approximately 60,000 net square feet. The major elements in the program are community use of spaces which include a Gymnasium, a Multi-Purpose Room, a Music Room, and an Academic Area which includes two kindergarten rooms, eight classrooms each for the primary and secondary grades, and various ancillary spaces. Support elements for these spaces include an Administrative Core for the entire school, and a Library-Media Center as a focal point for the secondary grades.

Photo: Gerard Myers

William-Emslie YMCA

Buffalo, New York

Client: City of Buffalo

Architect: Robert Traynham Coles, Architect, PC

Completed: 1982

This two-story structure replaced the Michigan Avenue YMCA, demolished in 1965. The building includes a pool and gymnasium on the first floor and a senior citizens wing on the main floor.

Photo: David Gordon

Operations Control Center and South Park Yards & Shops

Buffalo, New York

Client: Niagara Frontier Transportation Authority

Project Team: Corddry, Carpenter, Dietz and Zack, with Robert Traynham Coles, Architect, PC

Completed: 1983

These two projects were built to support the operations of the Buffalo Metrorail System. The project team developed a state-of-the-art maintenance facility and a computer facility that oversees system operations. This two-story building houses the computers that control Buffalo's rapid transit system. Located at the end of the system, the entire fleet of cars is serviced in the maintenance facility.

Photo: David Gordon

Lindbergh Center Station

Atlanta, Georgia

Client: Metropolitan Atlanta Rapid Transit System
Project Team: Ammann & Whitney; Robert Traynham Coles, Architect, PC
Completed: 1983

This was originally an open-cut station, but eventually became MARTA's headquarters, built up into an urban, covered, station.

Photo: Robert T. Coles

Health, Physical Education & Recreation Complex, Phase I - Alumni Arena

S.U.N.Y. at Buffalo, Amherst, New York

Client: State University Construction Fund

Project Team: Robert Traynham Coles, Architect, PC; Sargent, Webster, Crenshaw & Folley, Consulting Engineers

Completed: 1983

The 10,000-seat Field House/Core Locker is used for university-wide events, as well as for public events when used as a Convocation Center. It is the largest gathering space on the $1 billion campus. The complex includes handball and squash courts as well as other supporting facilities.

Photographer unknown

Health, Physical Education & Recreation Complex, Phase II - Natatorium

S.U.N.Y. at Buffalo, Amherst, New York

Client: State University Construction Fund
Project Team: Robert Traynham Coles, Architect, PC; Ammann & Whitney
Completed: 1987

The building contains a 50-meter pool, a 10-meter diving platform, and seating for 2,500 spectators. It was completed in time for the World University Games held in Buffalo, and received a Design Award from the National Spa and Pool Institute.

Photo: David Gordon

Providence Station

Providence, Road Island

Client: Federal Railway Administration

Project Team: DeLeuw, Cather/Parsons, Ammann & Whitney, Perry, Dean, Stahl & Rogers, Robert Traynham Coles, Baker & Conlon

Completed: 1984

The new railroad station of post modern design is located between the old railroad station and the historic Rhode Island State House designed by McKim, Mead & White. The one story building of white limestone, with a shallow dome reflecting the dome of the nearby state house, is sited over the relocated railroad tracks. The station plan is determined by radial lines from the capital dome. The project includes a 400-car parking garage under the station. The Project Team, headed by Skidmore Owings & Merrill (SOM), was awarded a Citation in the Progressive Architecture 30th Awards. Skidmore Owings & Merrill's manager for the northeast corridor railroad projects, of which the Providence Station was one, was Marilyn Jordan Taylor, who became the first woman Chairman of SOM, and later served as the Dean of the School of Design at the University of Pennsylvania.

Photographer unknown

Appendix C: Selected Projects 77

Frank Reeves Center for Municipal Affairs

Washington, D.C.

Client: District of Columbia
Project Team: VVKR, Devrouax & Purnell, Robert Traynham Coles, Architect, PC
Completed: 1986

As part of the District of Columbia Government's ongoing effort to improve the built environment of the inner city, the Frank Reeves Center for Municipal Affairs was built at 14th and U Streets, N.W. in the Shaw Urban Renewal area, site of the riots in 1968 after the assassination of Dr. Martin Luther King, Jr. The $35 million office facility symbolizes the City's commitment to this urban renewal effort and is intended to serve as a catalyst for further development in the 14th and U Street corridors.

Photo: Maxwell MacKenzie

Asarese-Matters Community Center

Buffalo, New York

Client: City of Buffalo
Architect: Robert Traynham Coles, Architect, PC
Completed: 1988

A one-story addition to the existing swimming pool, containing a gymnasium, lockers and Senior Citizens Wing, serves a depressed area near Buffalo State College.

Photo: William H. Siener

Rehab Treatment Center, Gowanda Psychiatric Center

Gowanda, New York

Client: New York State Facilities Development Corporation
Architect: Robert Traynham Coles, Architect, PC
Completed: 1990

This 35,000 square foot facility serves as the Town Center for the clients and staff of this upstate Psychiatric Center. Grouped around a central atrium are Gymnasium/Multi-purpose Room, Library, Auditorium, community Store and Cafeteria, Contract Workshop, Classrooms and Administrative Offices.

Photo: David Gordon

Human Services Office Building
Canandaigua, New York

Client: County of Ontario
Architect: Robert Traynham Coles, Architect, PC
Completed: 1992

This two-story building houses two hundred county employees, serving social service functions including child care and probation.

Photographer unknown

Ronald H. Brown Ambulatory Care Pavilion Harlem Hospital Center

New York, New York

Client: New York City Health and Hospitals Corporation
Project Team: Robert Traynham Coles, Architect, PC, URS Corporation
Completed: 1998

This 125,000 square foot, four-story facility serves the Harlem Community, with 250,000 patient visits each year.

Photo: Zbig Jedrus

City of Buffalo Telecommunications Center
Buffalo, New York

Client: City of Buffalo
Architect: Robert Traynham Coles, Architect, PC
Completed: 2000

The Apollo Theater, a former movie house, was converted into a telecommunications facility, providing state-of-the-art facilities for public educational and government access. It was also intended to be used for commercial productions, to help generate revenue that would go back into the building. At the direction of the City, the architect undertook the task of redesigning the facility to accommodate TV production capabilities. The result is an 18,000 sq. ft. facility that contains two TV studios, four private editing suites, a conference room, a classroom, and other amenities.

Photo: David Gordon

Frank E. Merriweather, Jr. Branch Library

Buffalo, New York

Client: Buffalo and Erie County Public Library, City of Buffalo

Architect: Robert Traynham Coles, Architect, PC

Completed: 2006

This new 20,000 square foot library is located in Buffalo's inner city near the historic Hamlin Park neighborhood. It replaces a nearby branch housed in a shopping center. The new library houses the African American Resource Center, a research component for the entire system. It is the focal point for this new facility. The architect was given the challenge of designing a library that was functional, yet, in its design, would become a symbol of the African American traditions of the community. The African village is the prototype for the library. It's an open community where villagers move freely from one house to another, often sharing meals and story telling. The program for the library calls for three large reading rooms, the African American Resource Center, and an auditorium seating approximately 150 persons.

Photo: David Gordon

APPENDIX D

AFRICAN AMERICAN ARCHITECTS and INTERNS

Employed by the Firm 1964 - 2004

African American Architects and Architectural Interns Employed by the Firm 1964 - 2004

Name	School	Year	License
Casimir W. Acholono	Buffalo	1971	
Boye Akinola	Buffalo	1987	Registered
Mel L. Alston	Buffalo	1968	Registered
Warren Ansley	Hampton	1977	
Ralph Arrington	Unknown	1979	
Tyrone Bradley	Southern	1981	Registered
Bruce Brice	Buffalo	1971	
Lisa Brown	Erie Community College	1987	
Dexroy Chism	Buffalo	1984	
Charles Davis	Buffalo	2000	
William Davis	Howard	1988	Registered
Patty Frazier	Erie Community College	1993	
David Gordon	Yale/Buffalo	1977	
Robert Gray	Buffalo	1987	
Donald Harris	Howard	1979	
James Heck, IV	Hampton	1980	
Obi Ifedigbo	Buffalo	1986	Registered
Van Johnson	Hampton	1974	
Baron Marshall	Buffalo	1992	
Ed Norris	Howard	1969	Registered*
Kisha Patterson	Florida A& M	1996	
Anne Perry	Syracuse	1987	Registered
Charles Rush	Howard	1964	Registered
Carla Singleton	Howard	1999	
Rishawn Sonubi	Buffalo	2004	
Robert Terrell	Buffalo	1987	Registered
Alisha Teruel	Buffalo	2002	
Kathryn Tyler	R.P.I.	1982	Registered
Michael Wright	Howard	1977	Registered
Mabinty Yilla	Buffalo	2002	

* Licensed prior to Employment.

APPENDIX E

PUBLISHED ARTICLES

Note: The articles in this section have been reproduced as designed and formatted in the original publications where they appeared. Permissions to re-print have been obtained from the respective authors, publishers and photographers.

This article first appeared in *Buffalo Business*, October, 1963.

An Architect Looks at Buffalo

BY ROBERT TRAYNHAM COLES, AIA

Architecture in the past has been the great chronicler of history. Through it, we can see the splendor and beauty of ancient Greece, the power and greatness of the Roman Empire, the luxury and excesses of the French monarchy. The great cathedrals, temples and tombs of past civilizations reflect the intensity and zeal of man's religions and, beyond that, the spirit of man.

What will future historians see when they look at American civilization and, primarily, its cities? What heritage will Buffalo, one of the great cities of mid-America, leave for posterity in this age of urbanness? Perhaps we should all look at Buffalo and try to see it as an architect views it. Most people see things as they are—and this is what was contemporary 50 years ago. An architect looks at things in terms of what they might and can be. In this way, we might better understand the city—what it is, what it can be, what it must be if it is to survive in the future. We also can learn to appreciate its beauty and to recognize its shortcomings.

The visual sensation of Buffalo, approaching the downtown area from Lake Erie or the industrial south and east, is most impressive. We see no great architecture nor are we intimately aware of the scale of the towers on the horizon, but we do recognize an unmistakable urbanness that is undoubtedly intensified due to the horizontality of the city itself.

Buffalo's temples are the smokestacks of Lackawanna's industrial complex and the grain elevators along the Buffalo River, the profiles of its great commercial banks, the isolated tower of the Niagara Mohawk Power Corp. But, perhaps, most impressive of all is the silhouette of City Hall, a symbol of political might which has put an indelible image on the city and its past history.

Each of these temples of modern man is different, but each tells us a great deal about Buffalo; for it is industry, commerce and politics that have made Buffalo the city it is today.

As we circle the downtown core and begin to see vistas of Lake Erie and the Niagara River, and look again at these towers on the horizon, we cannot but wonder why a city so blessed with such a splendid natural setting has literally turned away from what should be its greatest asset. Within the city, there is no visual recognition that a relationship exists between the city and its lakefront setting. The most impressive temple of them all—City Hall, representing the people—actually turns its back on an aesthetic and economic asset which other cities from Chicago to Rio de Janeiro have made a focal point and a thing of beauty. Sixty years after Chicago recognized the worth of its Lake Michigan setting, Buffalo finally is taking positive steps to redevelop its waterfront through urban renewal.

Before we move along the sidewalks as pedestrians, we must comprehend the pattern of the city. From above, the grid pattern of streets with the superimposed radial pattern converging on Lafayette Square is readily discernible. In the immediate downtown area, we see many voids in the horizon of towers that failed to reveal themselves from a distance. These are the daytime storage spaces of the bright metal carriages of this civilization's beings. We notice that the tall towers really are few. In the immediate distance, and for mile after mile beyond, the city basically is horizontal, with an occasional spire rising above the tops of stately trees that are conspicuously absent from the downtown area. There is a distant tower on the horizon: Central Terminal, now only a skeleton and tomb of the fourth major influence which shaped Buffalo, the railroads.

The closer we come to the city, the less strong are our first impressions of it. As we attempt to find the heart of the core area, we are surprised to find that its center actually is between two centers—McKinley Square, on which City Hall fronts, and Lafayette Square further east.

McKinley Square, a manicured symbol of political power, is practically inaccessible to the pedestrian. It is a forbidding space lacking all human scale; its great openness is also its greatest disadvantage.

Openness, in the city, should be for the pedestrian. Such a necessary and important relief from the dense, intense urban pattern is conspicuously absent from downtown Buffalo. What would London be like without its Trafalgar Square, Rome without its Spanish steps, New York without Bryant Park, Boston without its Common or Public Garden? Many American cities, in their future plans, have let the large department stores provide this space in the form of commercial malls, but I feel strongly that this is more a public responsibility.

Although overlooked in most downtown renewal plans, Lafayette Square offers great possibilities as a central downtown plaza and open space, if only the automobile could be removed. Why not give Lafayette Square back to the pedestrian, even if traffic must be routed around or under it?

We look further around downtown and see little other than broad sidewalks, plain buildings, gaudy signs, congested streets and a monotonous linear commercial development which offer little beauty, interest or relief to attract the pedestrian. Looking at the new Library, I wonder why it was not built in a taller, simpler form. And frankly, I miss the unusual shapes and forms of the old Library.

Efforts toward downtown renewal often have tended to forget the necessity for humanness in the city—a lesson I hope will be learned before it is too late. I think it is unfortunate that Buffalo's newer buildings have been set right on their property lines, showing no recognition of the great lesson of ground-floor openness illustrated so aptly almost 15

CITY HALL: The most impressive temple of them all

PHOTO BY FITZGERALD

years ago in New York's Lever House. Too many of today's new buildings are efficient, sterile towers of glass and aluminum that say nothing except that they are new.

Buffalo does have a rich architectural heritage which reveals itself as we move toward Shelton Square. This is the area where Louis Sullivan, the father of the modern office building, showed the world how a skyscraper should soar. His Prudential Bldg., erected at the turn of the century, is no ordinary building. This is a work of art . . . a piece of architecture. Shelton Square, as a pedestrian area, with the Prudential Bldg. and Erie County Savings Bank, is a magnificent historical complex which must not be destroyed in

NIAGARA SQUARE: Inaccessible to the pedestrian.

PHOTO COURTESY BETHLEHEM STEEL CO.

the name of progress. Will this message be lost to a population that stood almost mute in 1950 when the Larkin Terminal Warehouse Bldg.—a masterpiece built in 1905 by America's greatest architect, Frank Lloyd Wright—was demolished?

Other than local homes done by Wright, notably those on Soldier's Pl. and Jewett Pkwy., there is perhaps only one other piece of outstanding architecture of the modern era in Buffalo—Kleinhans Music Hall, by the late Finnish master, Eliel Saarinen. The recent addition to the Albright-Knox Art Gallery is a handsome building on a glorious site, but it makes its primary focus a glass-walled auditorium while suppressing magnificent art in a windowless basement. To me, the reverse should have been done.

Moving north along Delaware Ave., we are appalled by the great destruction being carried out in the name of redevelopment, the making way for something new, slick . . . and, often bad. We are mistaking newness for goodness, even to the point of possibly destroying the Wilcox Residence near North St., a house rich in history and the finest example of Greek Revival Architecture still standing in Buffalo.

It is alarming, too, to see the wholesale waste of land in the blocks between Allen and Summer Sts., the anti-urbanness in a section so close to downtown. We soon discover the small West Side squares nearby. Johnson Park has almost been destroyed; Day's Park still could be rehabilitated; Arlington Park is a rare jewel that—thanks to the Allentown Assn.—has been saved.

In wandering through these downtown neighborhoods, one sees much that could be saved; one wonders whether it might be better for Buffalo or any city to rehabilitate what it already has to attract its former residents back into the city, rather than to build at tremendous cost new towers on the horizon in the midst of blight and deterioration.

From the edge of downtown to the city limits and beyond spreads the multitude of individual frame homes—a few on generous lots, but most jammed so close together in monotonous rows that any space between is all but useless. Buffalo was developed much later than Boston, New York, Philadelphia and other eastern cities which recognized the masonry rowhouse as the urban home. One wonders why this type of dwelling was not adopted here. Was it because Buffalonians wanted to have their cake and eat it too, that they wanted to live in suburban homes in the city, forgetting completely that adequate urban land for such dwellings was not available?

We must recognize, as urban renewal advances in Buffalo, that the city is urban; that every great city is characterized by denseness, compactness, cohesiveness; that there never can be suburbia in the city—regardless of the reasons put forth. Unless these important facts are recognized, the crowded sprawl which has led to blight and decay in the city's residential areas will most certainly return.

Happily for Buffalonians, this residential pattern was in-

LAFAYETTE SQUARE: Great possibilities as a plaza

SHELTON SQUARE: A magnificent historical complex

DOWNTOWN: Amid gaudy signs, little interest or relief

An Architect Looks at Buffalo 93

KLEINHANS: Outstanding architecture of the modern era.

RESIDENTIAL BEAUTY: Wright-designed home in Jewett Pkwy.

terrupted by Frederick Law Olmsted. One of the greatest landscape architects and planners at the turn of the century, he developed the Back Bay Fens in Boston and, with others, also planned the great treed boulevards of Buffalo: Lincoln, Humboldt and Bidwell Parkways, Richmond Ave. and others that formed a cultural arc from the Museum of Science to Delaware Park, with its Art Gallery and Historical Museum and Zoo, to Kleinhans Music Hall.

But parks and parkways are useless to a people who are immersed in the automobile age. Delaware Park already has been bisected by an expressway, and the trees along Humboldt Parkway have been toppled by bulldozers preparing the new Kensington Expressway.

Only an indifferent society could permit this destruction to go on. The past has shown us that the decline of any city has been related directly to the rise of the automobile's popularity. Will we ever realize that the city and the automobile are incompatible, that the solution we see in more urban expressways and downtown parking is no solution at all? Rather than waste more millions, destroy more neighborhoods and drive more people from the city, we should study closely the new rapid transit systems being developed in Toronto, San Francisco or Stockholm and see how they can be applied to Buffalo.

If, thus far, we have seen little for which present and future historians can rejoice, perhaps a view of our educational facilities—which could be this civilization's cathedrals—will provide the inspiration. In the last 10 years, millions of dollars have been spent on public and private schools and college buildings. I look at the new Erie County Tech, D'Youville, Canisius, State College and State University and see too many structures which, to me, reflect a society which fails to recognize the inspiration of a beautiful building. Many of these buildings are new, all are structurally sound, but many are mediocre and some are even bad buildings. None possesses that aesthetic excellence that makes a building a piece of architecture. Is this because of a lack of money, lack of talent, or just plain apathy on the part of people?

Nature gave this region a rare beauty which should have served as an inspiration and a challenge to its planners and builders. We have yet to meet this challenge. Buffalo, today, has less beauty than many cities considerably less blessed by nature. It had (until very recently, at least) few new build-

PHOTO COURTESY BUFFALO & ERIE COUNTY HISTORICAL SOCIETY

THE LARKIN BUILDING: A masterpiece demolished.

ings. It still has little genuine architecture and a citizenry that seems content to stand aside while much of its existing beauty is systematically destroyed.

A recent symposium sponsored by the local chapter of the American Institute of Architects on "aesthetic responsibility" tried to focus on the real reason for ugliness in our city. Certainly, this city's temples of industry, commerce and government are partially responsible for making Buffalo what it is today. Beyond that, however, we must recognize that the city is the people, and that it can be no more enlightened or concerned than are its citizens.

And finally, although most architects might not want to admit it, we as architects must bear the responsibility for much of this ugliness. For supposedly, it is we who have the education, knowledge and taste to lead . . . and it is we who all too often have missed opportunities to lead.

In Buffalo, where the greatest works of architecture in the past have been done by outsiders, there has been a recent trend to again turn to nationally known architects to design the city's major new buildings. Marine Trust Co. has chosen Skidmore, Owings & Merrill of New York, who completed the Albright Knox Gallery, for the renovation of the existing main bank building and to design Marine's planned new downtown building. This firm also has been retained as campus designer of the State University of Buffalo. Perkins & Wills, of Chicago and White Plains, will do all future planning at the State University College at Buffalo. Max Abramowitz, of Harrison & Abramowitz of New York, who planned the Brandeis University campus and many of its major buildings as well as the Lincoln Center in New York, will build the new Temple Beth Zion. And Minoru Yamasaki, of Detroit, one of the greatest and most sensitive architects of the contemporary era, recently was retained by Manufacturers & Traders Trust Co. to design its new headquarters.

Soon, we may see new towers on the horizon that can properly be called "architecture."

There is hope that a city which inspired and encouraged both Wright and Sullivan to create masterpieces will recognize the need for sensitivity and awareness of beauty in the future. It must if it is to survive.

This is how an architect looks at Buffalo.   END

This article by Linda Levine appeared in Buffalo Spree in 1981.

Coles and the framework of the physical education complex of the University. The architect sees architecture in a broad context. Photo by Irene Haupt.

The Impact of an Architect: ROBERT COLES

BY LINDA LEVINE

Robert Traynham Coles has had a very special experience as an architect. Born and raised in a blue collar neighborhood in Buffalo, he is one of the few black architects in America. Becoming an architect was not nearly enough of an achievement for him, however. While he was shaping his concerns as a human being into the graceful forms of his architecture, he was also setting about to widen the vistas of the profession of architecture.

After Coles received his master's degree in architecture from M.I.T. and served his apprenticeship with two of Boston's major firms, he returned to Buffalo and opened his own architectural practice. He is known for the thoughtful relationships of spaces within his buildings, closely unified with the outdoors, as well as for the human values these structures express. The firm of Robert Traynham Coles, Architect, is a builder of playgrounds, subway and railroad stations, office buildings, housing for the elderly, recreation facilities, arts complexes, and schools. His is an architecture that focuses on the city and particularly the inner city where people assemble in amplest diversity to find a high quality of life. Coles observes that, from antiquity, people have assembled in cities to experience the level of civilization they require. He sees the city as the apogee of civilization, and he is respected as a civilizing architect.

The profession of architecture has traditionally been less than civilized, however, its doors remaining quite shut. So, moments when architects have worried about subtle and often idle aesthetic distinctions (how nostalgic postmodernism ought to be, for instance), Robert Coles has been crusading to create opportunities for minorities and women to enter the field of architecture and to remain in it. For years, he has been visible at a national level as an advocate for humanistic change. This year, his effectiveness in extending the frontiers for young people to become architects has won him high distinction. He has received the Whitney M. Young, Jr. Citation for 1981 from the country's major professional organization, the American Institute of Architects, in recognition of his contribution to an architecture of social conscience.

As a reforming architect, Coles has developed a deeply personal vision. It combines his definition of architecture as the utilitarian art and his awareness of the human desire for an aesthetic flow of spaces. And that fluidity is in harmony with an architecture of the future he envisions. He predicts that the private spaces we live in will become smaller, as the spaces we share will become larger. A clear illustration of that view is the downtown suite of his firm's new offices in the unlikely old world atmosphere of the Ellicott Square building. His own office, where this interview took place, is small while a shared central space is generous. The relationship of spaces is a hint of his more encompassing view of the city beyond. He foresees cities and buildings becoming denser, as cities once again become central to our way of life. The restrictions of space are not bad, however, in Coles' view. He believes that architecture is an art of constraints and that some of the best architecture has emerged from the sparest means.

With such vision, Coles has evolved into an unconventional architect. In all senses, he is an architect turned toward society. Consistent with the attitudes that have shaped him and made him a builder and social advocate is an encompassing perspective on how we might best live. He doubts, for instance, that the individual house on the single lot remains a valid architectural form for the future. He sees the private house, the suburban setting, and the sentimentality for mediocre houses of the past, as selfish and backward modes. Either we do not see or we are afraid to know that we live in a world of houses made in an era now dead. Coles has a vision of an exciting urban future, comprised not of the old solitary way of life but of shared housing in as yet unseen forms. But it is the sense of values underlying these forms that has brought to Coles his recent distinction.

There really is no precedent for the phenomenon of Robert Coles. As a man, he is witty, wry, sardonic, controversial, provocative and angry all in the same calm and dignified tone of voice. Prophetically, he began engaging in acts of advocacy for unpopular causes as soon as he set foot back on home ground. He moved deliberately into the black community where he could be an example to young people, such as he never had when he was young. Though there was an early black architect in Buffalo, by the name of John Brent, Coles was unable to gain from him a complete picture of what an architect was. While he was growing up he knew Brent, but Brent never actually had an architectural practice, as he never had the opportunity to develop one. He worked for other people, and for the city of Buffalo, designing such a building as the Michigan Avenue YMCA (torn down in the 1970s). So Coles had to develop his own vision of what an architect might be.

He got into architecture by a strange twist. "I think it was by an act of discrimination — and a bit of luck." He graduated from P.S. No.8 with grades too good to bar his admission to Hutchinson-Central Technical High School, where he was in an infinitesimal minority of black students. It was during World War II, and he wanted to study mechanical or electrical engineering, the glamour fields of the age of high technology, but was placed instead in a washout course called building design, which nobody wanted to study. By age 13 he was fairly expert with a slide rule and by 15 a formidable draftsman, having always been adept at drawing and with tools, and he discovered that building design was what he really wanted to do. He decided to go to college, which had never been on the horizon, and become an architect. A teacher tried to dissuade him by enlightening him about the world and suggesting he would have greater chances at the post office or in the ministry. But that was precisely the discouragement that Coles needed to be convinced he would be an architect.

Never having had a real black experience, as his mother thought he ought, he attended Hampton Institute, where his parents had gone, but he left disappointed with the academic standards. Still set on being an architect and getting the best education for it, he went to the University of Minnesota, where he majored in architecture and minored in political science. (He had declined to go to Southern Illinois, where he was also accepted, sensing it was too close to the South for comfort. He'd had enough of southern attitudes at Hampton.) To be able to afford graduate school, he went to work and then headed East to M.I.T. What he decidedly did not have either there or at Minnesota, where he was the only black student of architecture, was a black experience.

At M.I.T. he was awarded the Rotch travel prize by the Boston Society of Architects, enabling him to travel to Europe for a year with his wife, Sylvia, and their infant child to see architecture. Returning to this country, he kept a promise to live in Cambridge for a time, to take advantage of the cultural riches he'd never had the money for as a student. He apprenticed first to the firm that rebuilt Colonial Williamsburg, and then with the firm that succeeded Henry Hobson Richardson, the famous Victorian architect. To add to Coles' early success, his master's thesis became famous — a plan for the redevelopment of the Ellicott district in Buffalo — and he was invited here to oversee a project implementing the plan. It was a rare fate for a master's thesis. And it was the end of the ivory-towered life in Cambridge. Coles consciously chose to leave an ideal world for a real world and to buy land in a ghetto in Buffalo.

Involving himself in community life, he served at first in traditional ways and then in ways that hadn't been tried. He actively sought methods to end discrimination by the medical profession, in the early 1960s, as a member of a Western New York subcommittee of the U.S. Civil Rights Commission. As a result of the committee's work, the practice of segregated hospital wards ended, and wards began quietly to be opened up to all patients, black and white. During that period, on a different tack, Coles polled his neighbors on Humboldt Parkway for opinions on the proposed expressway that was to slice up the street. Perceiving that it would obliterate the neighborhood, he began to act. The fact that he was employed as an architect by the engineering firm that was designing the expressway might suggest, to some, a conflict of interest. To Robert Coles, it was simply one of the paradoxes of his life.

Little acts of advocacy grew into big ones. Coles began to look at architecture, less from the standpoint of buildings and more from the standpoint of people. He was well aware of riots occurring in Watts in Los Angeles and in Rochester and of turmoil on college campuses across the country. He became thoughtful about what he might do to prevent similar conflicts in his own city. Meanwhile, he served on a community committee of a poorly faring settlement house in the dismal air of Lackawanna when a new director was called in with a view to saving the place. The director, Richard Prosser, was to have a major influence on Coles' future as an architect. Prosser perceived in Coles a man with an unusually broad touch in the community, a traveler in a world that was economically, socially and racially mixed. He encouraged Coles to use his talents as an architect for improving the lives of people. Coles, recognizing he was in a unique position to try to unite poor people to act in their own behalf, was, by 1964, to become a committed voice for community reform.

The philosophy underlying the work that Coles began to do was quite simple. It said that the poor were without one of the two principal means of exercising various forms of control over their own lives. The only means open to them was to organize a political power base and demand that a percentage of the community's resources would reach them. The need for improved schools and housing, streets and neighborhoods was evident. The idea was to marry these needs at the grass roots level and, by collective action, to alleviate physical blight of the inner city and, ultimately, psychological despair. It was Cole's feeling that a city could have a lot of fine architecture, but without a peaceful social order, it could all go up in smoke overnight. He was just a little ahead of his time, and ahead of the architectural profession, in making the connection. He foresaw that without strong social foundations, physical foundations would be meaningless.

The early advocacy movement in Buffalo was successful, in Coles' estimation, in spite of forces of wealth and power in the city that legislated against it. Speaking straight out as always, he adds, his personal involvement in public controversy was probably threatening to people who may well have hired his services as an architect. But he held fast to his convictions, and his faith enabled him to take risks against all odds — risks even dangerous to his business practice. The more important thing was that he was beginning to see results, that collective action was helping to dispel some of the hopelessness and apathy prevalent in ghetto areas of Buffalo. Empowering the poor, and the middle class, was having its effect not only on the city but also on the architect. Coles later wrote, "Because he has the ability to see things as they can be, today's architect has a special task which goes beyond simply designing the physical environment. He must be an activist involved in the social and political life of the community." Looking back, Coles says there was a time he thought of himself as an architect by day and a social organizer by night. Ultimately he saw it was all of a piece, that he was becoming an architect and a person at the same time.

As his colleagues in the country have recognized, a long series of successes in advocacy can be traced back to the vision and courage of Robert Coles. He was a founder of BUILD (build, unity, independence, liberty, dignity), the action group spawned by a fund-raising arm that he initiated. BUILD, erected on the predominately black east side of the city, was closely followed by CAUSE, a parallel organization on the largely white west side, which has spun off into the United Citizens Organization. Coles patterned these groups after those of Saul Alinsky, the late social organizer and head of the Industrial Areas Foundation, whom he met through Prosser. Out of a common sense of purpose and friendship with Alinsky, Coles grew to be instrumental in uniting the most disparate of Buffalonians — city father to neighborhood worker — in cohesive goals and actions.

While his detractors were discriminating against him, as risky business, he was often asked for gratuitous architectural services, as the only minority architect in the city. If Coles saw any irony in this, he saw a good opportunity, as well. To meet the community's needs, he conceived of an organization that would provide comprehensive planning and design services at no charge. The key was to engage the volunteerism of the architectural profession. He invited the School of Architecture of the University of Buffalo and the local chapter of the A.I.A. to collaborate with him on this idea, now flourishing ten years later, in the name of the Community Assistance Planning Center. Deepening still further the frontiers of architecture into minority areas of cities and counties and the country, Coles helped to found the National Organization of Minority Architects. He was subsequently asked to oversee minority affairs in the national office of the A.I.A. in Washington, D.C., and accepted the post on the condition that he could continue to work one day a week in Buffalo. Coles' success, in all likelihood, is rooted in his ability to modestly step down when he feels he has served his use. Thus, he stepped out of his national post once it became clear that the growth of minority architects in America had begun.

For a host of successes, there had to have been a failure. And so there was. Coles' vision of a waterfront university in Buffalo, attracting shops and restaurants, density and diversity, was thrown overboard. He was a central figure on the committee for a waterfront university, promoting the idea of the city's regrowth in a most natural manner, preserving the best of the old buildings and interspersing them with the new. Coles is not alone, as countless others in hindsight see the correctness of that early vision, that great hope for Buffalo. But Coles, strong and flexible, is reshaping his vision of a civilized urban environment. At the same time, he has been one of the energetic planners of the Amherst campus of SUNY, and whether or not the plan ever materializes fully, one of the more dramatic and humane structures will be the health, recreation and physical education complex designed by Robert Traynham Coles. In the early stages, the dynamic complex now underway was a collaboration with Buckminster Fuller, whom Coles has known since days at Minnesota. Coles, not often one to look back, is nevertheless still regretful that there is no turning back.

A visionary, he is equally a pragmatist. Still searching for ways to open up the profession to the largest numbers of people, he remains active at a national level in a crucial concern of the inner city: housing. Additionally, he has broadly encouraged the concept of joint ventures, the collaborations of minority firms and majority firms on large projects. The significance is at least twofold. Since, in Coles' view, architecture is an art of the affluent, and the black community is not an affluent community, joint venturing gives blacks access to centers of influence and money, licensing them to be commissioned to do architecture of real worth. Secondly, the concept attracts firms to share their expertise. Clearly, architectural advocacy is by now a pattern of life for Coles, who practices what he preaches, that an architect "must truly be a revolutionary who sees his architecture as a broad movement to enhance the quality of life of urban man."

Architecture is all about urban life, he understands, and the profession ought to reflect the rich texture of that life. Still, only two percent of the country's architects are black and only one percent are female. Coles' own firm — with offices in Washington and projects underway there and in Boston, Providence and Atlanta — is half minority and half majority and likely to remain so. With the welcome mat out to women, the business end is in the professional hands of a woman with steady eyes and an unflinching style, Sylvia Coles. She is the firm's comptroller, and shares her husband's dedication to ideals.

Coles has made a quiet impact on his city, and continues to wield a power equivalent to the challenge raised by Whitney M. Young, Jr. at the 1968 national convention of the A.I.A. Coles sat in the audience, moved and inspired, as the late civil rights leader said, "you are not a profession that has distinguished itself by your social and civic contributions to the cause of civil rights, and I am sure this does not come to you as any shock. You are most distinguished by your thunderous silence and your complete irrelevance."

If Coles draws any attention to himself, it is for his unwavering steadiness, a quiet charisma. There is a side of him that likes solitude, sailing his boat on Lake Erie. But mainly he has chosen to be involved with people. He has taken the stance of a leader, going into the streets, finding out about human concerns. Yet his vision of a moral architecture has made no compromise with artistry. His design awards through the years will dispel any thought that he has had to exchange one ideal for another. He has had two ideals, a vision he has welded together. This year, his attainments have culminated in his being elected to the Fellowship of the A.I.A. Thus, Robert Traynham Coles, FAIA, becomes only the fourth architect in Western New York ever to win this honor.

To a humanist, honors show merely what he has been in his life up to now. Coles sees himself as an architect with a most human dream — of civilized urban life so vital to social peace. Architecture, he recognizes, is only the reflection of society's concerns at any time in history. In Greek antiquity it was the city, in Roman the palazzo, in the Renaissance the spirit of the cathedral. Today, it is the spirit of an idea. Coles draws little these days, thinking instead about what he might leave behind. He is building an idea, an institution he hopes will outlive him, a stairway to social justice. He was aroused by injustice many years ago and still sees an imperfect world. He thinks that we who are here, if we do nothing else, can make it a slightly better world.

EDITORIAL

This Guest Editorial appeared in the July 1989 issue of Progressive Architecture Magazine.

Black Architects, an Endangered Species

Architect Robert Traynham Coles, FAIA, comments on the vulnerability of black architects in practice and the declining numbers of blacks in schools of architecture.

What happens to a dream deferred -- does it dry up and die, like a raisin in the sun?

--Langston Hughes

IN 1968, five years after I started my own architectural practice, I attended the national convention of the AIA in Portland, Oregon. I was one of less than a half dozen black architects out of almost 4000 persons attending. It was here that civil rights leader Whitney M. Young, Jr., embarrassed the nation's architects by saying: " ... You are not a profession that has distinguished itself by your social and civic contributions to the cause of civil rights, and I am sure this does not come to you as any shock ... You are most distinguished by your thunderous silence and your complete irrelevance ... You are employers, you are key people in the planning of cities today. You share the responsibility for the mess we are in - in terms of the white noose around the central city. We didn't just suddenly get in this situation. It was carefully planned." Only a month later, in June 1968, the Report of the Kerner Commission, which studied recent urban riots, reported that " ... this nation is moving toward two societies - one black, one white, separate and unequal."

Last year, the nation celebrated the 20th anniversary of both of those events. The anniversary of the Kerner Report did not go unnoticed, and most reporting on the event indicated that it was a prophesy come true - that we had indeed moved toward two separate and unequal societies, in spite of all the civil rights legislation and rhetoric to the contrary.

In May of 1988, the AIA held its annual convention in New York, and this time almost 10,000 persons attended, but there was nary a word spoken about the 20th anniversary of the remarks by Whitney Young, Jr. And even though the event was held in the city with the largest black population in the country, and one of the largest groups of black architectural firms, no more than a score of black architects attended.

Between 1968 and 1974, spurred on by the words of Whitney Young, the AIA had mounted a major thrust to increase the number of blacks in the profession. Black architects were encouraged to join AIA and were elevated to major positions. Since 1968, four blacks have been elected AIA vice presidents. A minority architect scholarship program was established; educational programs were aimed at elementary and secondary schools to identify minority architectural students. Universities opened their doors to increasing numbers of black students and put in place support programs to ease their transition into integrated schools and an integrated profession.

Unfortunately, it all came to a screeching halt in the late 1970s, with the recession that swept the architecture profession. The pattern had been set in 1973 by President Nixon, who put a moratorium on low and moderate income housing, one of the mainstays of black firms.

Fortunately for black architects, Nixon's Secretary of Transportation was William Coleman, a black lawyer who initiated the most effective affirmative action program in public works by mandating that 15 percent of all funds for mass transit go to minority firms. As major new transit systems were built in several cities, black architects benefited. But President Reagan, elected in 1980, dismantled the remaining housing programs and drastically reduced federal funding for mass transit. This year, the U.S. Supreme Court set the future direction of affirmative action when it struck down a minority subcontracting program implemented by the city of Richmond, Virginia.

In the last two decades, the number of architects in the United States, according to Labor Department statistics, has roughly doubled. The number of female architects, less than 1500 in 1970, is approaching 5000. The number of black architects has grown from about 1000 to about 2000, remaining at about 2 percent of the total.

Minority enrollment in schools of architecture, which increased to almost 10 percent in

This Guest Editorial is condensed from a speech delivered in March at the University of Kansas, where Robert Traynham Coles was the 1989 Langston Hughes Distinguished Professor of Architecture and Urban Design. The original Langston Hughes lecture was published by the School of Architecture and Urban Design at the university. Coles is principal of his own firm in Buffalo, New York, and New York City. From 1974 to 1976, he was the AIA's Deputy Vice President for Minority Affairs, the highest staff position a black has held at AIA, and one that was not refilled. The opinions expressed here are not necessarily those of AIA's editors or management.

the late 1970s, has fallen to less than 5 percent, while female enrollment has increased from 10 percent in 1970 to more than 25 percent. The decrease in black enrollment is in evidence everywhere.

Black architects are an endangered species because those who are practicing are cut off from the mainstream of the society that controls building resources, just as the black community is isolated from these resources. Those who are in practice focus on public works because of the lack of access to private resources. As public construction shrinks, as affirmative action programs are struck down, as black political power diminishes in our urban centers, black architects are increasingly threatened.

This crisis threatens the profession, which in order to survive must begin to look like the society it must serve - a society which is becoming increasingly minority. It threatens our nation as well, for we can ill afford not to maximize the human resources that we have. We need the best and brightest to compete, regardless of race.

Robert Traynham Coles

Urban Waterfront and Public Access

An address on February 1, 1990 by Robert Traynham Coles, FAIA, for the Sam Gibbons Eminent Scholar's Chair Lectures in Architecture and Urban Planning, University of South Florida, Tampa.

In 1970, the Whitney Museum of American Art organized an exhibit by the Urban Development Corporation of New York State headed by Planner Edward Logue, entitled "Another Chance for Cities." The Urban Development Corporation was created in 1968 by Governor Nelson A. Rockefeller who distrusted the bureaucracy of existing government agencies, to arrest the physical decay in the state and mounted a major effort in creating new housing and new communities.

The exhibit's catalog, by Architect Robert A.M. Stern, is divided into chapters including Waterfront, Railyards, Downtown -- those major elements in our 19th century cities.

The chapter on Waterfronts states:

> What made the cities and towns in America has also destroyed them. The 18th and 19th century waterfronts and waterways were exploited for shipping cargo, transporting people and accumulating industry. On such activities, cities and towns survived. Used, exploited, but not considered a resource of permanence whose eventual function might change our waterways have become fouled, our waterfronts decayed.

> Along rivers and ocean ports, the edge of the city has become a platform for storage, for waste, for private commerce, for uncrossable rail and road conduits. Instead of diversity and shared use, bleak similitude has set in, the edge of the land lost to most of the people most of the time.

> In America, waterways have been historically places of serious commerce, and little else. At occasional celebrations devoted to themes of progress and national vitality, such as the World's Columbian Exposition of 1893, Chicago's waterfront land was transformed for popular enjoyment. But expositions are not permanent, and the lessons of delight learned at them are generally forgotten in our national passion for industrial ascendancy.

> Today, certain older industrial and shipping cities like Pittsburgh, Boston, Philadelphia, New York and smaller towns like Savannah and Buffalo are recognizing that the way beyond blight for their waterfronts lies in the direction of fundamental change in use, that the edge of the city, of the town, that unique spot where water encounters land, where climate changes, vistas open, that spot so long the service entrance of our towns, the back alley of our cities, is entering a new age. Recently, with hesitancy, with probing, through immense technical effort and public education, waterside development and redevelopment has been under consideration for recreation, for promenades, for parks, for housing, for citizens' use and enjoyment.

Post Industrial Cities in the rust belt are rediscovering their waterfronts. Public access has become a major concern as the former industrial sites are being sought for housing and commercial uses. How these new developments can thrive and still insure that there is adequate public access in the former Rust Belt cities can give direction to the new cities of the south, like Tampa, so that they, too, may rescue their urban waterfronts.

America's greatest Landscape Architect, Frederick Law Olmsted, who designed Central Park in New York, the Fenway in Boston, and Golden Gate Park in San Francisco, did extensive work in the late 19th century in many cities including Buffalo. He pointed out the special significance of Buffalo's lake and riverfronts:

> Buffalo owes its importance as a city to its position on Lake Erie. It has in Lake Erie really great natural scenery. It has no other and, can have no other to be compared with it in value.

Buffalo's entire history and existence was dependent upon its location on the waterfront. Situated on the eastern shore of Lake Erie at the mouth of the Niagara River, it was a major trading center for Native Americans, and then the later American settlers.

With the completion of the Erie Barge Canal in 1825, which extended its waterfront to the Atlantic Ocean, Buffalo became a major transshipment point for raw materials from the heartland of America that were needed in the eastern population centers. The early fur and lumber trade in the area was supplanted by the growth of the grain industry in the late nineteenth century; and Buffalo thrived as scores of lake boats, now driven by steam, brought tons of raw materials to its shores.

The railroad replaced the canal as the major transportation link to the east, and the city became the largest railroad center, behind Chicago, in the world. Refinements in the production of steel and the discovery of major iron ore deposits in mid-America continued the growth and development of

Buffalo's industrial waterfront.

At the turn of the century, the Scranton Steel Company moved its major steel producing facility to Lackawanna, just south of Buffalo. Later, acquired by the Bethlehem Steel Corporation, it grew to become the fourth largest steel mill in the world, employing more than 25,000 people during World War II.

At the turn of the century, Buffalo was like many of the new cities of the south and southwest in the post war years -- Houston, Dallas, Tampa, and Phoenix, doubling its population every ten years. Although fortunes were made on the waterfront, new development in the area turned its back on its natural heritage. In the great building boom of the late twenties, major new buildings were erected in the City -- a gigantic City Hall, which, though located close to Lake Erie, turns its back on it, and a huge new passenger terminal for the New York Central Railroad, which even today – now abandoned, -- sits miles away from the waterfront, on the edge of the City. The only new major development on the waterfront in the post World War II era was a 1,000 family, eleven-story high, low income public housing development which was later converted to middle income housing.

World War I and II and the post war eras were boom years for rust belt cities like Buffalo, and their waterfronts thrived. With the development of new highways, the trucking industry replaced railroads. However, with the construction of the St. Lawrence Seaway, there was no need to transship materials at Buffalo as ocean vessels could now reach into America's heartland, and by-passed the city. War-ravaged plants in Japan were replaced by efficient new steel mills, and soon it was cheaper to ship scrap and iron ore to the far east, convert it to steel, and ship it back to this country, than to produce it here.

Several magical opportunities for development on the waterfront were ignored by Buffalo. Although a planning study had glowing recommendations for Buffalo's waterfront, the State chose to build its new billion dollar Graduate Center campus in suburban Amherst, twelve miles away, --- now the fastest growing city in New York State. Erie County, whose seat is Buffalo, built its new 80,000-seat stadium – home of the Buffalo Bills – in suburban Orchard Park, miles away from the city and anything else for that matter.

Buffalo, which was the 14th largest City in the United States before World War II, reached its peak population of 600,000 just after 1960. In the two decades that followed, it lost half of its population in the industrial decline that saw major development in the south, southwest, and west sap the city of its industrial strength. In the decade between 1970 and 1980, Buffalo followed St. Louis and Cleveland in a population decline approaching twenty five percent. The City lost almost fifteen percent of its population in the last decade and is now only the fiftieth largest city in the country.

The closing of the giant Bethlehem Steel complex and other plants on the Lake Erie shore in the early eighties, and the awareness of environmental concerns has led to a new interest in the waterfront, and the city. As new recreation and housing developments appear on the waterfront, the question of public access becomes a major concern.

A new state funded agency, the Erie County Horizons Waterfront Commission was established in 1988 to oversee the development of the almost 100 mile waterfront in Erie County.

The Inter-municipal Cooperation Agreement that created the Horizons Waterfront Commission States:

The Parties jointly and individually recognize the paramount importance of Erie County's 90 miles of waterfront to the revitalization of the region; and

The Parties recognize the unparalleled opportunities for recreational, housing, commercial, industrial, transportation and other uses which are available on the waterfront; and

The Parties recognize that the Lake Erie and Niagara River waterfront in Erie County is contained within the boundaries of five towns and three cities; and

The Parties mutually agree that the only way to properly plan and implement the multi-year, multi-million dollar development and redevelopment of the waterfront is through a unified planning and implementation process; and

State aid is critical to the implementation of a unified, comprehensive and regional waterfront plan; and

The Parties agree that the best and most efficient way to develop public policy, coordinate public and private development, and to use public resources on the waterfront is through a joint, cooperative process; and

The Parties agree that a single regional master plan for the entire waterfront is a critical element in the development of the waterfront; and

It is proposed that a new public benefit corporation named the Horizons Waterfront Commission, Inc., hereinafter referred to as the "Commission", will be formed as a subsidiary corporation to the Urban Development Corporation of New York; and

The purposes and powers of the Commission include, but are not limited to:

1. The development, adoption and updating of a Master Plan for Erie County's waterfront,

2. Receiving and distributing state, federal and other funds to carry out waterfront development projects.

3. The designation of a lead agency to carry out specific development projects,

4. The coordination of the activities of all governmental entities in the development of the waterfront,

5. Acting as a developer of last resort when a development project cannot be effectively and appropriately carried out by a local entity, and

6. Coordinating and focusing private investment and development efforts: and

The Commission is to be assisted by 18 ex-officio, non-voting members who shall include representatives from the economic development agencies from each of the parties, and other County wide public agencies, business groups and certain state agencies.

How Buffalo and Erie County deals with public access to its Lake and riverfront can be a guide to the waterfront development of the new cities of the south, southwest, and west. Buffalo, has been given a second chance to do the right thing. As Santayana said, --- "those who do not know history are subject to repeat it." The knowledge of how to achieve public access with the growth and development of the waterfront should be explored as a major research effort. It has given cities like Buffalo an opportunity to preserve their waterfront heritage. This is truly "another chance for cities ".

Robert Traynham Coles, FAIA

Robert Coles and Lewis Harriman, with poster reading "Happiness is a Waterfront University", July 1986. Photo: Sylvia Coles

My Experience as an African American Architect, and Prospects for the Future

A talk by Robert Traynham Coles, PC, at Howard University, February, 2001

INTRODUCTION

I grew up in Buffalo, New York, where I have practiced architecture for almost forty years. Because Buffalo was an Industrial City, the schools were geared to the industry in the area. Most children went to two years of a vocational high school, then began working nights in industry, and probably left school before graduation for a job in industry. I went to the Technical High School that enrolled students from all over the city. Today, it would be called a magnet school. Out of 1800 students, less than a dozen were black. Because my entering grades were so high, they had to admit me even if I was black, but they shunted me into a course called Building Design that had few enrollees during World War II when no building was taking place. I took to Building Design like a duck takes to water, and by the time I was a sophomore, I was leading my class and began to think of things beyond High School, and decided that I wanted to be an Architect. I began doubling up on my courses so that I could go to college. I recall this incident vividly. One day, my teacher took me aside and said, "Bob, you're wasting your time trying to be an architect. There are no opportunities for Negroes in that area. Why don't you go to the Post Office, become a social worker, or a minister". Can you imagine how a young person would feel if someone like a teacher whom you held in high esteem would come up to you and say you can't fulfill your dreams for the future? Tears welled up in my eyes but I gritted my teeth and said that I would be an architect, and the best darn architect that I could. I graduated 3rd in a class of 300 in 1947 and now have the highest name recognition of any architect in western New York. I went on to graduate from the University of Minnesota and M.I.T., and am now completing 38 years of practice. I come to speak to you today as an activist. Today, I would like to tell you about some of the personal acts of advocacy I've been involved in and how they might affect our future.

AN ENDANGERED SPECIES SPEECH

Eduardo Catalano was an Argentine Architect who came to this country in the fifties and taught first at North Carolina State and then moved to Cambridge and M.I.T. I got to know him at M.I.T. when I was a graduate student. He built a house in Raleigh, North Carolina which was a hyperbolic paraboloid--a curved concrete roof, with all of the functions of the house underneath. It was a great success among the architectural profession, if not the public. Eduardo, as I call him, said once that some architects build many houses before they are successful, but I built only one. Perhaps you can say the same about my "endangered species" talk. In the winter of 1989, I was Invited to the University of Kansas to become the Langston Hughes Professor of Architecture. I had been a critic at Kansas since 1969 when the new Dean Charles Kahn invited me there after we met in Portland, Oregon, where Whitney Young had spoken to the AIA Convention. Langston Hughes actually spent his boyhood days in Lawrence, and to commemorate his death, a Professorship had been established that would rotate between the various colleges. 1989 was the year that the College of Architecture would have the Professorship. I suspect that they looked around, and the only black architect that they remembered was me, so they invited me back to the University. I would be in residence at the University periodically during the year. With Lawrence, Kansas forty miles away from Kansas City, you had to focus on what was, or was not there. And what was missing were the number of black students that I had seen here over the two decades that I had been going there, both in the entire University and also in the architectural school, where there were less than a half dozen out of almost 600 students. I was asked to do an inaugural lecture, and I decided to talk to the group about my own practice, and the plight of black architects everywhere. The title of my paper was, "The Practice of Architecture in a Post-Industrial City: The Profile of a Black Architect-An Endangered Species". I told John Morris Dixson, also a M.I.T. graduate and then editor of Progressive Architecture Magazine, about it, and he decided to excerpt it as a guest editorial in his magazine, entitled, "Black Architects: An Endangered Species". Some of my colleagues were aghast at the idea that we were an endangered species, and said, Bob sees the glass as half empty, and it is in reality, half full. Many of my colleagues in the profession do agree with me now.

DIRECTORY OF AFRICAN AMERICAN ARCHITECTS

Apparently, someone was listening to what I said in my "Endangered Species" speech. Bradford Grant, now Director of Hampton University's Department of Architecture, and Dennis Mann, Professor of Architecture at the University of Cincinnati's Center for the Study of the Practice of Architecture, were intrigued by the statistics concerning the number of African American architects. In my speech, I said that the number of black architects had grown from 1,000 to 2,000. They began to assemble materials on the subject, conducted a nationwide survey, and published their findings in 1991 in a Directory listing all of the known African American Architects by state, as well as those who were teaching. Their survey established that the number of African American Architects was closer to 1,000 at that time, and are perhaps no more than 1500 today. Interestingly, the number of African American women in the profession was under 50 in 1991, but has tripled to almost 150. A second Directory of African American Architects was published in 1996, and also, a new report, "The Professional Status of African American Architects". In a recent telephone conversation with Dennis Mann, he told me that he has attended every annual meeting of NOMA. His recent survey information lists about 1350 African American Registered Architects, of which 122 are female. Another interesting statistic is that there are perhaps 1300 African Americans in Architectural degree programs, of which 45% of these or 585 are in historic black schools. 265 of these are at Howard University. In looking at the statistics for Howard Graduates, between 1975 and 1985, of 85 graduates, 75 became registered. Between 1985 and 1995, out of 95 graduates, only 19 are registered. I will discuss that later.

HOW WHITNEY YOUNG AFFECTED MY LIFE

Have you ever looked back upon your life and tried to pinpoint what was the deciding moment, or person you think that shaped your life? As I think about my life, the late Whitney Young had a major impact upon it. I first met Whitney Young when I went to college at the University of Minnesota in 1949, and he was head of the Urban League in St. Paul. A social worker, he had attended Graduate School at Minnesota and had started his career there. The University of Minnesota had a history of educating future black activists. Roy Wilkins, the longtime Executive Director of the NAACP, graduated from the University in 1923. The Journalist, Carl Rowan, graduated from the Journalism School, and former Cleveland Mayor Carl Stokes honed up on his negotiating skills while playing bridge in the student union at the University. Whitney Young served as Dean of the School of Social Work at Atlanta University and later moved to the National Urban League as its Executive Director. In the mid-sixties, this country was torn by racial strife, and cities like Newark, Detroit, Los Angeles were on fire, and death and destruction were all around. The American Institute of Architects invited Whitney Young Jr. to be the keynote speaker at their 1968 Convention in Portland, Oregon. My first AIA Convention was in St. Louis and the only reason that I went was that I received an award for a project. To me, like many of my younger counterparts, the AIA was a stodgy organization controlled by conservative old white men. But the 1968 convention was on the West Coast and it would be an expense paid vacation. Knowing that Whitney Young would be speaking, I made it a point to attend, and sat in rapture as he challenged the Institute to do something about the urban crisis.

You are not a profession that has distinguished itself by your social and civic contributions to the cause of civil rights, and I'm sure that this does not come to you as any shock -- you are most distinguished by your thunderous silence and your complete irrelevance. You are employees, you are key people in the planning of our cities. You share the responsibility for the mess we are in -- in terms of the white noose around the central city. We didn't just suddenly get this situation. It was carefully planned.

You could have dropped a pin in the hall at the conclusion of his address, and then the applause began, first slowly, and then louder and louder. As I watched the AIA mobilize in response to Whitney Young, I got involved. Kansas Dean Charles Kahn invited Whitney Young to the University of Kansas as a guest critic, along with Architect Charles McAfee of Wichita while I was teaching a class there, and I got to know Whitney Young, this soft spoken man who died too soon in a swimming accident in Africa in 1970, just two years after his AIA address. I have attended every AIA Convention since Whitney Young's address in 1968. Later, I organized a Community Design Center in Buffalo with Howard graduate Charles Rush, now an Architect in Albany. In response to Whitney Young's call to get involved, I later became the first and only Deputy Vice President for Minority Affairs for the AIA, designed the Whitney M. Young Jr. Health Center in Albany, New York, and in 1981 was awarded the Whitney M. Young, Jr Citation from the AIA. Last year, with the suggestion by the 1999 Citation Winner, Charles McAfee, I encouraged the AIA to do an in depth article about Whitney Young Jr. in the newsletter, AIArchitect.

THE PHELPS STOKES INITIATIVE

At the College of Fellows luncheon in 1989, just after the Endangered Species editorial was published, and encouraged by my classmate, former AIA President Randy Vosbeck and my friend, Robert Marquis, I had the opportunity to address the luncheon on the diminishing number of African American architects who were entering the profession. As a result, the AIA convened a Task Force on African American entrance into the profession. The Task Force, led by New Yorker William Rose, Vice Chancellor of the College, was composed of approximately 25 people. It met in late January of 1990. Dr. Andrew Billingsley, former Academic Vice President at Howard University and President of Morgan State, with whom I spent my first two years at Hampton, was the keynote speaker. The following is the major finding of the Task Force in a report released in March of 1990.

The indisputable conclusion is that African Americans are not only turning away from careers in architecture, but that the process of declination is beginning disturbingly early in the lives of young African

Americans. Even presuming a quick and successful reversal of current trends of participation, it is likely that the potential contributions of a generation of African Americans may be lost or at best diminished to the development of architecture as an art and a profession.

The report was given to the AIA's Diversity Task Force to implement, and unfortunately, little was done, probably because the Diversity Task Force is too diverse. I was elected to the College of Fellows Executive Committee in 1991 and was also appointed Associate Professor at Carnegie Mellon University. Chancellor William Rose also served on the Board of a small college whose former President, Dr. William Le Melle was then head of the Phelps Stokes Fund in New York City. He believed that African Americans should be teachers so that they can become beacons and attract students in the schools. After several meetings with Dr. Le Melle, the heads of the Architectural Schools at Howard and Hampton considered joining with Carnegie Mellon in a pilot program. There was some skepticism on the part of Howard, but Hampton University did join, and two of its graduate students did enroll at the University. Unfortunately, with a Masters in their hands from Carnegie Mellon after two years, the students were attracted back into the profession and did not continue on for their Doctorates and eventual faculty positions. The initiative ended when both sponsors mistakenly thought that the other had the resources to fund the half million dollar program

THE URBAN AGENDA

In 1993, when I became Vice Chancellor of the College of Fellows, riots occurred again in our cities after the Rodney King verdict. It appeared that the time was ripe for a major initiative to focus on the problems of our cities and what architects could do to remedy them. At the June 1993 AIA Convention, about two dozen Fellows met after lunch with me to discuss how a major thrust for an urban agenda could be developed. In the summary of the meeting, I stated:

My concern is that the inner cities of our nation are becoming more and more isolated, and that the population---increasingly black, brown, and now yellow---are becoming more estranged from the mainstream of society. The hostility that we saw in the recent uprisings in Los Angeles, Atlanta and Miami should have been a wake up call for action, and yet the call has not been heeded, as the affluent suburbs that surround our cities have turned their backs on the problems that we must face and confront if we are to survive as a nation.---It is my intention to make the Urban Agenda the focus of my tenure as Chancellor of the College of Fellows, but I need your help.

Nice try, but it didn't work. My fellow Fellows on the College of Fellows Executive Committee didn't see the need for an Urban Agenda, and the effort failed.

CHANCELLOR OF THE COLLEGE OF FELLOWS

Another result of the Endangered species speech was my being elected in 1991 to the Executive Committee of the College of Fellows, the first African American to hold such a post. During the first two years as Secretary I worked with Chancellors William Rose and Robert Marquis on the Phelps Stokes Initiative. Robert Marquis, the first Jewish Chancellor of the College, whom I had met in 1964 in St. Louis at my first AIA Convention and who supported me as the first African American Chancellor of the College of Fellows, was enthusiastic about the Stokes initiative and was disappointed to determine that they were unable to fund the effort. Also, as I mentioned earlier, my effort to develop an "Urban Agenda" was discouraged. But as Chancellor of the College, I had the responsibility to pick the Keynote Speaker and the person to give the Invocation at the Convocation Dinner. I selected Politician/Architect Harvey Gantt, former Mayor of Charlotte to give the Keynote Speech, and Educator/Architect, Dr. Sharon Sutton, to give the Invocation. Both are committed advocates. In March of my Convocation year, I suffered from depression, and had to resign as Chancellor of the College of Fellows. However, the Keynoter and the Invocator were already in place. It was with great joy that I traveled to Atlanta to attend the Convocation Dinner, to have Sharon Sutton have the audience all clasp hands as she emotionally moved the attendees, and to be challenged by Harvey Gantt in a speech as powerful as Whitney Young's. In hindsight, perhaps that was all I could do as Chancellor of the College of Fellows.

THE NATIONAL ORGANIZATION OF MINORITY ARCHITECTS

I believe that the most creative thing that African American Architects have done is form the National Organization of Minority Architects. There was much discussion about the name of the organization and ourselves---minority architects, black architects, African American Architects. Minority won out because there was the expectation, never realized, that federal grants would be forthcoming. In 1968, at Portland, Bob Nash was over there, Leon Bridges was somewhere else, DeNorval Unthank somewhere else, and Bob Coles and Ben McAdoo somewhere else, but in those days, we acknowledged each others existence with a nod, and went on our way. At Detroit, it was different. It was an east coast location and more of us were there, many who came from cities like Detroit, Chicago, Cleveland, and Buffalo as well as Washington. When someone from Architect Nathan Johnson's Detroit office asked us to visit their office, we jumped at the opportunity. The word spread, and soon most of the African American Architects at the convention were there. We looked at their work, discussed our work, and more importantly, the problems we had in getting work. A group of those there decided to meet in the Bahamas in the winter --you could tell what the pattern of African American architects would be from the locations that they picked. Based upon the two informal meetings, a call was made for a third meeting in Chicago in June 1972, and of course, it was at the Playboy Club. This was at the same time that the Peoples Political Party was meeting in Gary at the run down Central High School. Each meeting was held to bring African Americans together, but the venues were contrasting. Because of the lack of communication between members, I started a Newsletter, and later served in every office of NOMA except President, probably because the members thought they couldn't control me in that office. After almost ten years of involvement with NOMA, I turned my attention to the AIA. Dennis Mann, who published the Directory of African American Architects, and I talked about NOMA. He feels that the older NOMA members and the founders should stay with the organization. It may be that the founders should be a continuing resource, but it is necessary for new leadership to emerge and invigorate the organization from time to time, and this should be a continual process.

COOPERATIVE VENTURING

I served as the first and only Deputy Vice President of Minority Affairs for the AIA between 1974 and 1976. My task was to increase the number of African Americans in the profession and the Institute. In reality, because of the depression in the profession, what I had to do was to develop programs that would keep African American Architects in the profession. I worked directly under Architect Robert L. Wilson, from Stamford, Connecticut, who was the first African American President of the Connecticut Society of Architects, and who also formed the New York Coalition of Black Architects, and was the third AIA Vice President. Bob was the enterprising idea man, and I was the implementor. We decided to explore Joint Venturing between majority and minority firms, and had a day long conference at AIA Headquarters with 100 firm principals, 50 who were majority architects like Weldon Beckett, and 50 who were minority architects like the late Leroy Campbell. Leroy was the key note speaker and he gave a paper that could be used as a standard for Joint Venturing today. That conference was valuable in enabling African American Architects to circumscribe some of the pitfalls, and the pit bulls of practice as we went on to other major projects. In 1976, when I left the AIA to return to practice, I was asked by my classmate, Randy Vosbeck to join VVKR, then a major Washington area firm, but declined and suggested that we joint venture on work in the Washington area. That relationship led to the largest black/white joint venture till then with the design of the Frank Reeves Center for Municipal Affairs at 14th and U Street with VVKR, Devrouax and Purnell, and my firm. Paul Williams and Hilyard Robinson worked in joint venture on a housing project in the thirties. I understand that Robert Nash and Leon Bridges had a very successful Joint Venture on the Baltimore Railroad Station, and that Donald Stull and David Lee in Boston are working with Michael Willis in San Francisco. There are also some very successful African American family practices, such as McKissack and McKissack in Nashville, Whitney and Whitney in Cleveland, Wendell Campbell in Chicago and Mort Marshall in Reston. Most recently, my firm with William Davis and Jack Travis, three African American Architects with large egos entered into a competition to design a $10 million recreation club in Harlem. At the completion of the competition, we all agreed that the experience of working together was extremely valuable. Although we didn't win the competition, we did learn that we can and must begin to work together.

THE BENJAMIN LATROBE FELLOWSHIP

Last fall, the College of Fellows announced a $50,000 grant that will be used to research the future of the profession. What good is this profession, I began to think, if it does not begin to look like the society that it has to serve. I wrote Robert A. Odermatt, the 2000 Chancellor of the College of Fellows, the following, suggesting that an African American be selected. I suggested that some subjects that an African American Latrobe Scholar might want to explore are:

- The profession is seeking the best and the brightest to move forward in the twenty first century. How can the profession develop more creative ways to open the doors for more African Americans to become involved?

- The profession continues to turn its back on the urban areas of our country that are in dire need of assistance and especially the inner city areas. What creative approaches can be developed to involve the profession in making our cities truly livable for all of its citizens?

We need an African American Latrobe Fellow who can bring to the forefront the rich talent that African American Architects have that has not been fully utilized or recognized by the Institute or the profession just as African American Benjamin Banneker's contributions to Washington are little known. Hopefully, a jury representing the racial diversity of our profession will make the selection of an African American, who have, for the most part, been left out of the mainstream of the profession. The annual $30,000 Rotch Traveling Scholarship Competition, administered by the Boston Society of Architects, which I won in 1955 when the stipend was $5,000, has just had their second African American winner in 45 years, an African American woman who is now traveling in North Africa. There have been talks of increasing the stipend because of the recent success of the stock market. I've told the Rotch Committee that because of the limited number of African Americans in the pool, they may have to wait another 45 years unless they spend the surplus of money they earned over the last decade in developing programs that will increase the number of African Americans.

THE SCHOOLS

I had always wanted to combine practice with teaching and the opportunity came in 1990 when I was asked to join the faculty at Carnegie Mellon University by John Eberhard, former Dean at Buffalo and later head of the AIA Research Corporation. As a full time Associate Professor, my job was to bring the real world to the students, but I found, to my amazement, that the students did not want the real world. As one of the students wrote, "I came to school to dream". Well, that's fine until you have to interface with the profession. If the only skills that you bring are dreams, it isn't going to cut the mustard. I served on a visiting committee when Jerry Lindsey was Dean –probably thirty years ago. He wanted to make Howard the Harvard of black schools with a four-two curriculum, and I told him that it should not be imposed on black students who have limited funds for an education and need to be given skills quickly so that they can enter the profession. I understand that you have a new Dean who may wish to make you more theoretical, and I would resist it if you can, regardless of what Harvard, Yale and Princeton are doing. I understand that fewer students who graduate are licensed. This should be a warning to you. In Buffalo, I have two Howard students from that era, both female, who are not licensed, and several from Hampton who are in the same category. There are some successful models of early entrance into the profession that could be emulated. The University of Cincinnati has a cooperative program that requires students to work every third semester. In England, students must leave school after the fourth year and work for a year before returning for their final two years. The advantage of this early entry into the professions is that you can learn real skills, and more importantly, you can see what the profession really is and decide whether you want to enter it.

THE PRACTICE

Now this is where I have some expertise. In 1968, five years into my practice, my firm was awarded the commission to design the $25 million Physical Education complex at the State University of Buffalo, partly because of the graduate thesis on recreational facilities that I did at M.I.T. in 1955. From a base office in Buffalo, our firm has designed projects in Atlanta, New York City, Providence, and now Dallas. An African American engineer friend of mine said recently that if you want to be successful in this business, you have to come back wearing a skirt or a turban. In some ways, affirmative action that assisted us several decades ago, especially with the Mass Transit programs, is working against us as all minorities are grouped together. White women have been very successful in entering the school and the profession. Today, almost half of the entering freshmen are women, and the graduating classes are one third female. The other problem that we face is territorial. Most of us work on public projects in urban areas; we have no access to the suburbs since we have little political base there. As private work shrinks in the suburbs, many majority firms are moving into major public works projects in the cities. If there is an effective affirmative action policy like that which exists in Atlanta or Washington, African American firms have an opportunity. In my own practice, I learned how to get on an airplane to another city where there is work. I'm not sure about what happens in Texas where John Chase seems to be on all of the teams. Perhaps John can give us a clinic on "How To Get Work". I do know, however, that regardless of the pitfalls of practice, architecture is the most satisfying thing that I could do.

THE FUTURE

If we are to move forward in this profession, we are going to have to do it ourselves. The world doesn't understand why we need to make this profession look like the society that it has to serve, but we do, and we are going to have to get involved. We need more black advocate architects like Robert Johnson Nash to stand up to society and say, " We belong here just as you belong here. Try to keep us out." No one made more of a difference to this profession than Bob Nash. In Portland, in 1968, he too was inspired by Whitney Young, and he became an advocate. We need more of you to catch on fire so that those who follow up can enter the mainstream of this profession. Our future has got to be based upon the past and the legacy that so many African American Architects have left, beginning with Paul Williams, who was our idol. Lest we forget, there is an honor role of African American Architects that we should never forget who are no longer with us. But their memory is. And this list is not limited to the following:

Paul Williams - the first modern pioneer who paved the way for all of us.
Howard Mackey - Howard University's great teacher of a profession of black architects.
Louis Fry, Sr. - a great teacher and architect who recently died.
John L. Wilson - a distinguished architect and Whitney Young Citation winner from New York.
Robert J. Nash - the soul of black architects, who died two years ago.
Elmer McDowell - a spunky architect from the Virgin Islands who served on the AIA Board.
Lonnie Adkins - a graduate of Hampton where I first met him, and who practiced in the Twin Cities.
DeNorval Unthank - From Eugene, he was one of five black architects in Portland.
James C. Dodd - a Californian, he also served on the AIA Board.
John Sutton - a graduate of the University of Kansas, he practiced with LeRoy Campbell.
William Moses - head of Hampton, he won the Virginia Competition for the 1939 World's Fair.
Henry Livis - a fellow Hamptonian, he was also a distinguished practitioner.
Hilyard Robinson - one of the pioneer design architects, he also taught at Howard.
Robert Kennard - a California giant who died too soon. Now his daughter heads the firm.
Walter Blackburn - had he lived, he would have been the AIA's first African American President.
Kenneth Groggs - one of the pioneers of NOMA, and a great public servant in Illinois.
Leroy Campbell - a distinguished leader of NOMA and his firm, Campbell Sutton.
William Brown - a NOMA founder who practiced in New Jersey.
Robert Perkins - from New Orleans, he was one of the early founders.
Joyce Whitley - the sister of twin architects James and William, she was the team's planner.
Harry Simmons - a savvy Brooklyn architect who died tragically while piloting his own plane.
And **John Brent,** a mostly unknown architect from Buffalo who built the city's "colored" YMCA.

Robert Traynham Coles, FAIA

BUFFALO BY ARCHITECTURE
BUFFALO MODERN

by Kelly Hayes McAlonie

Photo by Kc Kratt

This article by Kelly Hayes McAlonie appeared in the Fall 2011 issue of Buffalo Spree Home magazine. Photography by Kc Kratt.

Given that the City of Buffalo came of age in the late 1800s and experienced tremendous growth in the decades that followed, most of our housing stock dates to these periods. Fortunately, quality design and construction during this time left Buffalo with a legacy of high-caliber architecture from this era. By the mid-twentieth century, it seemed our luck had run out: Very few homes exist here that represent this modern era that were not mass produced. Those that do should be treated with great care as they represent an important albeit tumultuous time.

The post-World War II era brought prosperity to the United States and with it, a changed perspective on city living. The notion of a new, single-family dwelling with a large yard and white picket fence captured the imagination of Americans and drove young families into the suburbs throughout the fifties and sixties. This shift in housing trends not only impacted architecture and landscapes but also urban planning. With most jobs still located in city centers, the new wave of suburban commuters wanted quick and easy access to work. Coupled with President Eisenhower's interstate highway program – which aimed to connect the country with ribbons of roadways – the country was experiencing an unprecedented housing and highway construction boom.

In New York State, one of the chief advocates for suburban emigration was Robert Moses, who oversaw the construction of many of the state's urban highways. Though he met opposition in New York City when urban activists stopped the construction of the Lower Manhattan and the Mid-Manhattan expressways, his urban philosophy was embraced in Western New York, and prompted the construction of Interstate Highways 190, 290, the Kensington Expressway, the Scajaquada Expressway and, of course, the Robert Moses Parkway in Niagara Falls.

Meanwhile, the single-family houses being built for the users of these highways were significantly smaller than they'd been before, and appealed to young, newly married couples who wanted the American dream – on a tight budget. Many of these houses were designed by developers, but there were a few architects who influenced residential design at this time.

Opposite page: Architect Robert Coles, FAIA, and his photographer wife Sylvia designed this living room in their modern home. Above: The front entry is obscured from the street. One enters through a modern courtyard, extending the interior to an urban garden. Below: The living spaces open to the back terrace and garden. Modern sculpture accents the property inside and out.

114 Buffalo By Architecture

Frank Lloyd Wright developed a series of homes in 1936 that he called "Usonian." Wright believed in the moral and political values exemplified by home ownership and believed that well-designed, tasteful dwellings would produce a happier, more harmonious and enlightened society. With these houses, he intended to develop an architectural language and construction method for the production of affordable, simple, well-designed houses. In the 1930s, forties, and fifties, many Usonian houses were built throughout the country. In the 1950s, Wright developed the Usonian Automatic home, which was composed of three-inch thick modular building blocks that buyers could use to build their own homes at a lower cost (although most clients chose to work with a contractor instead).

The original and Automatic Usonian houses were one-story with no basement or attic, and had concrete, radiant heated floors, natural wood walls, built-in furniture, brick masonry piers, and fireplaces. Floor plans were streamlined to accommodate changing patterns of family life and entertainment. Several multi-purpose zones allowed for family activities, and the kitchen was often paired with the bathroom to create a service core that replaced Wright's hearth in his Prairie Style designs. The built-in dining area and living room were located off the kitchen and the bedrooms occupied another more remote zone. Consistent with Wright's design philosophies evident in the Prairie style, the connection to the outside environment was also important in the Usonian house. The idea of building spaces to accommodate the needs of the users is consistent with the "not so big" idea of today and was, in fact, its precedent.

Carl Koch, FAIA, was another architect who influenced residential design in the middle of last century. A Cambridge, MA-based architect who was educated at Harvard and had studied under Walter Gropius, Koch was intensely interested in creating affordable, well-designed houses for the middle class. Inspired by the Usonian houses and the International Style – an early century precursor to modern architecture that featured rectilinear forms, plane surfaces devoid of ornamentation, and open interior spaces – Koch developed the Techbuilt House in 1954. These houses were designed with prefabricated components that could be custom assembled to create houses that were unique to the needs of the client but could benefit from the affordability of mass production.

The Techbuilt wall and floor panels were typically eight-by-eight feet and the windows were designed and sized to fit within the eight-foot grid. Koch designed the houses with post-and-beam construction that allowed for the large expanses of glazing. The exterior design was characterized by a single gable roof, large plate glass windows on the gable ends, and deep eaves. Like Wright homes, Techbuilt houses often were designed around a common family "hearth," featured built-in furniture systems – prefabricated in this case – and celebrated the connection to the outside through large expanses of windows and outdoor rooms. Techbuilt became a phenomenon and Koch ultimately developed twenty-two different models within the system that ranged from $14,000 to $70,000. The houses won design awards from the American Institute of Architects in the 1950s and are now listed on architectural surveys by the National Trust.

To meet demand throughout the country, Carl Koch & Associates worked with franchised builders located near their clients to erect the houses as per the architectural documents. In Cambridge, Koch enlarged his staff of architects to design and manage the projects through construction. During this time, Koch hired a young architect from Buffalo named Robert Coles.

In 1958, Bob Coles, FAIA, was given the opportunity to return to Buffalo to build his MIT Master's Thesis project, a Recreation Center on Buffalo's East Side, which would later be named for John F. Kennedy. For a short period of time, he commuted between Buffalo and Cambridge, before permanently resettling in Buffalo and establishing a practice. During this time, the city was making plans to build the Kensington Expressway and Coles identified a site on Humboldt Parkway, in the Hamlin Park neighborhood, that would become available for purchase. In 1961, when families were leaving Buffalo in favor of the surrounding suburbs, Bob built a contemporary house for his young family in the heart of the city.

The Coles house is modeled on the Techbuilt prefabricated system and the principles that Wright used in designing the Usonian homes; indeed, the windows, wall system, and floor panels all were fabricated in the Techbuilt factory on Long Island. However, with its flat roof, horizontal windows and white painted brick facade, the house appears to take its cues visually from the International Style rather than its Techbuilt precedent.

Approaching the house, one passes through a front court that serves as an outdoor vestibule and kitchen garden, and protects the entrance from the sounds of heavy Kensington traffic. A large Jack Solomon sculpture dominates the court, which is also defined by a lattice fence that was inspired by a project designed by Paul Rudolf.

The house is divided into three zones: the studio, the lower floor – where the eat-in kitchen and children's rooms are located – and the upper floor where the living/dining room, master bed room, and guest room are found. Like Wright and Koch, Coles sited the house to take advantage of the natural environment. As a result, few windows look to Humboldt Parkway, but the house opens up to the back yard which is a modern garden oasis with an amphitheater back terrace.

A raised balcony overlooks the back yard from the living room. Strategic window placement yields remarkable passive solar qualities, keeping the house cooler in summer and warmer in winter.

The interior finishes were all installed by Coles and wife Sylvia and most are original. Of particular note are the Danish cork floor and Douglas Fir ceiling beams. The house is also a showcase for artwork – paintings, sculpture, and photographs – including some by Sylvia, who is a photographer. Built with ideas that withstood the test of time, the home feels contemporary, even fifty years later.

Modern architecture has regained popularity in residential design in the past few years, with magazines such as *Dwell* advocating that we build houses to meet our current lifestyles and environmental sensibilities. Building smaller homes and exploring construction delivery options such as prefabricated systems and sustainability are but a few examples. But these got their start fifty years ago in suburbs throughout the United States and at least one neighborhood in transition in Buffalo.

Kelly Hayes McAlonie, FAIA, LEED AP is an architect and the Director of the Capital Planning Group at the University at Buffalo and 2012 President of the American Institute of Architects New York State. She is a frequent contributing writer to Buffalo Spree and Buffalo Spree Home.

Arthur O. Eve, NYS Assemblyman and Robert Traynham Coles, at a reception for Eve, Buffalo, NY, 1993.   Photo: David Gordon

Acknowledgments

MANY persons have influenced my life and contributed to my career in architecture, with some figuring most significantly.

Ammann & Whitney Engineering firm, New York City, gave me the opportunity to assist in the design of the Providence, Rhode Island Railroad Station on the Amtrak Northeast Corridor, the Lindbergh Center MARTA Station, and the natatorium at the HPER Complex.

Lawrence Anderson, FAIA, Dean of the School of Architecture and Planning at MIT, who received the Topaz Award for exceptional educational achievements, encouraged me to believe in myself and my design capabilities.

Louis Angelikis, AIA, Los Angeles architect, was a classmate at the University of Minnesota's College of Architecture and Landscape Architecture. While students, and working together in his father's firm, he and I designed the Richfield, Minnesota Bank, our first major architectural project.

George K. Arthur, Buffalo City Council President, was actively involved in my selection to design the Jesse E. Nash, Jr. Health Center, and the Ellicott Homes project (now demolished), two early projects. He continued to lend advice on minority issues.

John Brent, AIA, distinguished himself by becoming Buffalo's first Black architect. A graduate of the Tuskegee School of Architecture, we met through our families' friendship. He gave me helpful advice regarding schools of architecture.

Elizabeth DiFranco, whom I first met at MIT, was my chief designer, involved in the HPER Complex and the Frank Reeves Center, the Townsend Dental Building and Bidwell Post Office in Buffalo.

James Dobson, President, Catholic Inter-Racial Council, Rochester, New York. His advocacy led to my commission to design the Urban Park Housing Project in Rochester.

Richard K. Dozier, PhD, Dean Emeritus, Robert Taylor School of Architecture and Construction Sciences, Tuskegee University; former Professor & Associate Dean, Florida A&M University. He wrote the Foreword for the 1996 Exhibit of Black Architecture at the Burchfield Penney Art Center in Buffalo, which included a number of my projects.

William L. Evans, longtime Head of the Buffalo Urban League, mentored my MIT Master's thesis, "Community Facilities in a Redevelopment Area—A Study and Proposal for the Ellicott District in Buffalo, N.Y."

Arthur O. Eve, Deputy Speaker, New York State Assembly. His activism in advancing minority participation led to my commission to design the HPER Complex.

Lewis G. Harriman, Jr., was the Vice President of Community Affairs at M & T Bank, in Buffalo. A longtime board member of Calasanctius School, his community interests were varied and all-encompassing, including spearheading the light rail rapid transit system. My involvement with Lew included working together in the drive for a waterfront university and stadium.

H. Robert Hodge, AIA, a graduate of George Washington University and Harvard School of Design, joined my staff as a consultant and worked on various projects including the HPER Complex.

David Lewis, FAIA, from Pittsburg, was also a Kemper awardee. The founder of Urban Design Associates, he mentored me during the years I served as Associate Professor at Carnegie Mellon University.

Robert Marquis, FAIA, San Francisco architect whose social activism was reflected in the design of buildings such as San Francisco's St. Francis Square housing. We first met at the 1964 national AIA Convention in St. Louis. He became my advocate, encouraging my involvement in the AIA, leading to my becoming Chancellor of the AIA's College of Fellows in 1994.

Arthur McWatt, St. Paul, Minnesota historian, was another friend I met while attending the University of Minnesota. His history of St. Paul is a classic.

Jesse Nash, Jr., LLD, Buffalo community activist and educator, and long-time head of Buffalo's Model Cities Program, was my first Buffalo friend. We met each other in 1962. He gave me good advice regarding my designs, and we taught each other's classes several times.

Edward B. Norris moved to Buffalo from Boston to assist in the design of the HPER Complex. Later, he was Executive Director of the Community Planning Assistance Center. He left Buffalo to head the Design Center at the University of New Mexico in Albuquerque.

Kathryn Prigmore, FAIA was on my Washington staff. She later became an award-winning architect, with over thirty years in private practice. She also served as Associate Dean at Howard University's School of Design. She was a recipient of a National Women of Color Lifetime Achievement Award.

Richard Prosser, Buffalo Social Worker and Community Activist hired me when he headed the Friendship House community center in Lackawanna, New York. I designed the new center, and during that time Prosser introduced me to Saul Alinsky and to social activism.

Marshall E. Purnell, FAIA, who became the first Black president of the national AIA in 2007, was a partner in the firm of Devrouax and Purnell.

Harry Quinn, P.E., Manager of DeLeuw, Cather & Brill Engineering, the firm that retained me to design the John F. Kennedy Center, my first Buffalo project. The completed Center was named "one of the best buildings in Buffalo designed in all time" by the Western New York Chapter of the AIA.

Ralph Rapson, FAIA, also a recipient of the Topaz Award, was the Dean of the Minnesota School of Architecture and Planning. I came to know him through my Rotch Travel letters. I was inspired by his overcoming a physical handicap to become a leader in the field of architecture and design.

Miriam Reading, Chautauqua Institution Board Member was a social activist, instrumental in my commission to design the Sample Memorial Playground at Chautauqua. The Playground was cited by the New York State AIA for Design Excellence.

Charles E. Rush, Jr. was my first intern architect. He left my office to head Buffalo's Community Planning Assistance Center (CPAC). He played a major role in the planning of the University at Buffalo's Health, Physical Education and Recreation Complex (HPER).

Lucas Smith, from Minneapolis, who attended the University of Minnesota with me, became a friend and socializing influence, unfortunately dying at an early age.

Dr. Sharon Sutton, FAIA, an outstanding Seattle educator and activist architect, developed a platform to increase the opportunities for minorities in the profession. She delivered the invocation at my inauguration as Chancellor of the AIA College of Fellows.

Wilbur P. Trammell, Chief Judge, Buffalo City Court. He helped secure one of my first Buffalo projects, the Lanigan Field House. When he ran for Mayor of Buffalo in 1989, I managed his campaign.

Jack Travis, FAIA, activist architect, educator, and writer, edited the 1991 publication, *African American Architects in Current Practice*, which included my firm. As an educator, he did a superb job in relating the Black experience to his students.

Gail Viner, AIA, was the first of my Washington, DC staff. She figured in the design of the Lindbergh Center MARTA Station in Atlanta.

R. Randall Vosbeck, FAIA, Washington D.C., another classmate at the College of Architecture and Landscape Architecture, was later awarded the Kemper Citation by the American Institute of Architects (AIA). Thanks to his nomination, I was elevated to Fellowship in the AIA in 1981. His firm, VVKR, associated with Devrouax and Purnell, another Washington firm, and mine to design the Frank Reeves Center for Municipal Affairs in Washington, DC.

David Walsh, AIA, was the New York City project manager for the Ronald H. Brown Ambulatory Care Facility at Harlem Hospital, and with his skills contributed to the building's success.

Robert Traynham Coles, FAIA

Index

A

activism
- activism outside the firm, 21
- activist defined, 18
- Alinsky, Saul, and ESCO founding, 22–23
- architecture and activism one and the same, 18
- architecture and Coles' activism, 29
- Coles' civic activism, 42
- commitment to social activism, 6
- ideals of the activist architect, 49–50
- oppostion to UB's Amherst campus, 24–25
- Sharon Sutton: "architects as agents of change", 52

Adams, Michael, historian, xiii, xiv

advocacy
- agenda furthered by election as Chancellor of College of Fellows, 41–42
- as an 11-year-old, 3
- Coles named AIA Deputy Vice President for Minority Affairs (1974), 1, 29, 102, 108
- collaboration with Dr. Sharon Sutton, 52–53
- discrimination in the Medical Profession, 22
- efforts to increase no. of minority architecture students, 37–38
- organized a campus chapter of the NAACP, 4
- Prosser's influence, 21
- remains focused on advocacy, 49

African American community, Buffalo, NY, xiv, 10, 22, 23, 44, 45

Afro-Centric Architecture, 46–47

AIA, xiii, xiv, 1, 8, 16, 21, 24, 25, 26, 27, 29, 30, 32, 35, 37, 39, 40, 41, 42, 48, 49, 50, 51, 52, 53, 54, 56, 57, 64, 66, 68, 101, 108, 109, 110, 117, 118, 124

American Institute of Architects. *See* AIA

Amistad, xi, 43, 44

Ammann & Whitney Engineering, 30, 32, 73, 75, 76, 117

Anderson, Lawrence, FAIA, 5, 9, 117

Angelikis, Louis, AIA, 4, 117

Apollo Theater, City of Buffalo Telecommunications Center, 45, 62, 83

architects
- African American, 18–19, 87
    - Brent, John, AIA, xiv, 4, 10, 50, 51, 58, 98, 112, 117
    - Dozier, Dr. Richard K., AIA, vii, xiii, xiv, 3, 26, 50, 51, 52, 117, 124
    - Evans, William L., xiv, 9, 117
    - Marquis, Robert, FAIA, 38, 45, 108, 109, 117
    - Nash, Robert, AIA, 26, 110
    - Norris, Edward B., 18, 29, 87, 118
    - opportunities blocked by racist assumptions, 29
    - Purnell, Marshall E., FAIA, xiv, 32, 53, 54, 78, 110, 118
    - Rush, Charles E., Jr., 17, 18, 26, 87, 108, 118, 124
    - Travis, Jack, FAIA, 38, 49, 110, 118
    - Whitney Young's career shaped by, 26–27
    - Wilson, Robert, 29, 30, 110
- Anderson, Lawrence, FAIA, 5, 9, 117
- Angelikis, Louis AIA, 4, 117
- Brown, Clinton, FAIA, 10, 17
- Catalando, Eduardo, 5
- Hodge, H. Robert, AIA, 117
- Johansen, John, 5
- Kahn, Charles, FAIA, 37, 107, 108
- Kahn, Louis, 5
- minority
    - Coles as AIA Deputy Vice President for Minority Affairs, 1, 26, 29, 99, 102, 108, 110
    - encouragement by Dr. Wilbert Le Melle, 38
    - minority/majority collaboration, 30
- Rapson, Ralph, FAIA, 4, 5, 118
- Rudolph, Paul, 5
- Shibley, Robert G., FAIA, 53
- Vosbeck, R. Randall, FAIA, 1, 4, 32, 41, 49, 52, 53, 55, 108, 110, 118, 124
- Walsh, David, AIA, 118
- Women
    - Bethune, Louise Blanchard, xiii, 51, 57
    - Prigmore, Kathryn, FAIA, 32, 41, 118, 124
    - Sklarek, Norma, FAIA, 39
    - Sutton, Dr. Sharon, FAIA, 41, 42, 52, 53, 109, 112, 118
    - Viner, Gail, AIA, 118
    - Washington, Roberta, FAIA, 38–39
- Yamasaki, Minoru, 5, 95

architectural education
- attracting minority students, 52–53
- disappointment with SUNY at Buffalo, 40–41
- encouragement by Le Melle, 38
- expanded role to recruit minorities and women, 35
- faculty appointment at Carnegie Mellon University, 35
- Hampton Institute, xiii, 1, 3, 4, 13, 98
- Langston Hughes Distinguished Professor of Architecture and Urban Design, 37, 102
- MIT, 1, 4, 5, 6, 17, 115, 117
- recommendation for Technical High School, 39
- Rotch Traveling Scholarship, 6, 7
- University of Minnesota, xiii, 1, 4, 32, 48, 49, 57, 98, 107, 108, 117, 118

architectural styles
- International Style, 5, 115
- Mid-Century Modern, 3, 9

architecture, minority access to profession
- absence of African Americans in the profession, 18

roadblocks despite academic achievement, 4
SUNYAB Architecture school a vehicle for attracting minorities to the profession, 40
Arthur, George K., 43, 44, 117
Asarese-Matters Recreation Center, 61, 79
awards, 56–57
Award of Merit for Coles residence, 49
First Award, Certificate of Merit for the Sample Memorial Playground, 49
Homes for Better Living, 8, 16, 49, 56, 67
medals, 48

B

Berlyn, Mr. and Mrs. Gerald, residence, 16, 17, 60
Bethune, Louise Blanchard, xiii, 51, 57
Bidwell Station Post Office, 35, 61, 94, 117
Black American Museum & Cultural Center, 29, 60
Brent, John, AIA, xiv, 4, 10, 50, 51, 58, 98, 112, 117
Brown, Clinton, FAIA, 10, 17
Buffalo, NY
African American community. See African American community, Buffalo, NY
Public Schools
New Elementary School No. 40, 60, 70
P.S. 8, 3
Technical High School, 3
BUILD (Build, Unity, Independence, Liberty and Dignity), 23, 99
Burchfield Penney Art Center, xii, 50, 51, 58, 117

C

Carnegie Mellon University, 35, 37, 38, 39, 40, 52, 109, 111, 117
Catalando, Eduardo, 5
CAUSE (Coalition for Action, Unity and Social Equality), 23, 99
Civil Rights movement, 18
serves on US Civil Rights Commission sub-committee, 22
Whitney Young, Jr., civil rights leader, 25–26
Clarkson, Max B. E., Graphics Controls President, 24
Coleman, William Thaddeus, Sec'y of Transportation, 1975-77, 27, 101
Coles, Darcy, 5, 6, 7
Coles, Sylvia (nee Meyn), iii, iv, 5, 7, 9, 13, 18, 20, 22, 26, 30, 34, 36, 38, 40, 41, 43, 44, 50, 53, 98, 100, 105, 116
Committee for an Urban University, 24–25
community renewal
"An Architect Looks at Buffalo", vii, xi, 13, 24, 32, 91–95
Coles' architecture creates positive urban experience, 10
Diana Dillaway interviews Coles for her book, 44
Merriweather library - a community gathering place, 46
construction technology
affordable housing using newer materials, 13–16
Coles studies building design, 3
Mid-Century Modern, 3, 9
proposal to offer technology courses at city campuses, 39
Techbuilt pre-fabricated homes, 8–9
unique design of Coles' home, 10–11

D

Design Diaspora, Burchfield Penny exhibition, xii, xiii
DiFranco, Elizabeth, 117
discrimination
discouraged from pursuing architecture, 4
experiences in youth, 3
Housing Discrimination in the Boston Area, 5–6
serves on Study of Discrimination in the Medical Profession, 22
subject of FBI surveillance, 5
diversity
Coles objects to AIA diversity initiative, 52
greatest diversity in cities, 13
promoted by Phelps-Stokes, 41
promoting Ethnic and Gender Diversity at UB, 53
Dobson, James, 117
Dozier, Dr. Richard K., AIA, vii, xiii, xiv, 3, 26, 50, 51, 52, 117, 124

E

Ellicott Neighborhood Advisory Council/UDC Housing Project, 60
Eppolito, Mr. and Mrs. Charles, residence, 17, 60
European Influences, 10
Rotch Traveling Scholarship, 6–7
Eve, Arthur O., 116, 117
exhibitions, xii, 2, 36, 50, 58

F

Frank E. Merriweather, Jr. Branch Library, iv, 1, 45, 46, 47, 50, 51, 62, 84
Frank Lloyd Wright, xiii
Frank Reeves Municipal Center, Washington, D.C., xiv, 31, 32, 34, 53, 61, 78, 110, 117, 118
Friendship House of Lackawanna, 21, 49, 56, 60, 66, 118

G

Gowanda Psychiatric Center, Rehab Treatment Center, 35, 61, 80

H

Harlem Hospital Center - Ronald H. Brown Ambulatory Care Facility, 32, 37, 42, 43, 62, 82, 118
Harriman, Lewis G., 18, 24, 105, 117
Health, Physical Education, and Recreation Complex, SUNY Buffalo, 17, 18, 30, 32, 33, 61, 74, 75, 111, 118
Historically Black Colleges and Universities, 40
historic preservation, 32–34
Hamlin Park Historic Preservation Study, 42
historic architecture in Europe, 7
rehabilitate vs. re-create, 13
Hodge, H. Robert, AIA, 117

HPER. *See* Health, Physical Education, and Recreation Complex, SUNY Buffalo
Human Services Office Building, County of Ontario, 35, 61, 81

I

inner cities, 10. *See also* urban blight
International Style
    an early proponent of, 5
interns
    African American interns employed 1964-2004, 87
    Charles Rush, Coles' first intern architect, 26
    hiring for the long term, 54
    proud of minority and women interns, 52
    staff reduction in 1990, 37

J

Jesse E. Nash, Jr. Health Center, 60, 117
JFK Recreation Center, xiii, 1, 2, 9, 10, 12, 13, 60, 61, 64, 115
Johansen, John, 5
Johnnie B. Wiley Pavilion Offices, 42, 62
joint ventures, 30, 32, 34, 35, 49, 53, 61–62, 72–78, 82, 100, 110
Joseph J. Kelly Gardens Housing for the Elderly, 1, 14, 16, 49, 56, 60, 67

K

Kahn, Charles, 37, 107, 108
Kahn, Louis, 5
Kigutu Health Center, 46, 47, 62

L

Le Melle, Dr. Wilbert J., 38
Lewis, David, FAIA, 117
Lindbergh Center Station (MARTA), 30, 32, 61, 73, 117, 118
Lownie, Theodore, 16

M

Marquis, Robert, FAIA, 38, 45, 108, 109, 117
MARTA Station, Atlanta. *See* Lindbergh Center Station (MARTA)
McCall, H. Carl (SUNY Board Trustee), 41
McWatt, Arthur, 118
mentoring
    Coles, a mentor for young architects, 51
    Coles gets Fellow Award for Mentorship, 52
    firm serves a wider purpose, 18–19
    Phelps-Stokes Fund provides mentoring for students, 38
Michigan Avenue YMCA, xi, xiv, 4, 10, 22, 71, 98
Mid-Century Modern Style, 3, 9
minorities in architecture. *See* architects: minority
Moorjoy, xi, 43, 44

N

Nash, Jesse E. Jr., LLD, v, xi, xiv, 22, 44, 50, 60, 117, 118
Nash, Robert, AIA, 26, 110
National Organization of Minority Architects. *See* NOMA
New Elementary School No. 40, 60, 70
Niyizonkiza, Deogratias (Deo) Burundi Village Health Works, 46
NOMA, 26, 30, 35, 108, 110, 112
Norris, Edward B., 18, 29, 87, 118

O

Operations Control Center, Buffalo, 32, 61, 72

P

Phelps-Stokes Fund, 37, 38, 40, 41
prefabricated components, use of. *See* construction technology
Prigmore, Kathryn, FAIA, 32, 41, 118, 124
Prosser, Richard, 20, 21, 22, 24, 26, 32, 118
Providence Railroad Station, 30, 61
Public School 128 Design, Queens, NY, 45, 62
public spaces, philosophy of
    humane public spaces, 13, 17
        private spaces should become smaller, public spaces larger, 10, 46
Purnell, Marshall E., FAIA, xiv, 32, 53, 54, 78, 110, 118

Q

Quinn, Harry, P.E., 118

R

race relations. *See* diversity
    Amistad mission to promote, 43
racism
    "did not rent to colored", 6
Rapson, Ralph, FAIA, 4, 5, 118
Ravin, Dr. and Mrs. Joseph, weekend house, 60
Reading, Miriam, 118, 124
residences architected by Coles
    Berlyn residence, Worcester, Mass, 16, 17, 60
    Coles home at 321 Humboldt Pkwy, 9, 11, 49
    Eppolito residence, Orchard Pk, NY, 17, 60
    Sterling Forest, Techbuilt house, 8, 56, 60
    Wright/Evans residence, Attica, NY, 16, 17, 60
Richardson, H. H., xiii
Richfield State Bank, 4
Rockefeller, Nelson A., 24, 103
Rudolph, Paul, 5
Rush, Charles E., Jr., 17, 18, 26, 87, 108, 118, 124

S

Saarinen, Eero, 5, 93
Sample Memorial Playground, 15, 16, 49, 56, 60, 68, 118
segregation
    "did not rent to colored", 6
Shibley, Robert G., FAIA, 53
Sklarek, Norma, FAIA, 39

Smith, Lucas, 117, 118
social justice
    11-yr-old Coles gets justice after discrimination, 3
    non-discriminatory housing law, 6
Solomon Sculpture Court, 14, 16, 17, 60, 116
South Park Yards & Shops, 32, 61, 72
State University of NY at Buffalo, 17, 18, 23, 24, 25, 28, 30, 32, 33, 39, 40, 41, 50, 53, 61, 74, 75, 94, 95, 99, 111
suburbanization
    cautions against suburbanization of the city, 13
    new SUNYAB campus in suburban Amherst, NY, 23–25
Sullivan, Louis, xiii, 92
SUNY at Buffalo. *See* State University of NY at Buffalo
Sutton, Dr. Sharon, FAIA, 41, 42, 52, 53, 109, 112, 118
    Coles' collaboration with, 52

T
Techbuilt homes, 8, 9, 115
Townsend Dental Clinic, 16, 60, 65, 117
Trammell, Wilbur P., 118
Travis, Jack, FAIA, 38, 49, 110, 118

U
UB. *See* State University of NY at Buffalo
University at Buffalo. *See* State University of NY at Buffalo
urban agenda, 41, 54, 109
urban blight, 21–22, 34
urban design
    Apollo Theater project, 45, 62, 83
    civilizing urban spaces, 7, 10
    Coles pholosophy, 13
    Committee for an Urban University, 24, 25
    Community Planning Assistance Center (CPAC), 1, 25, 26, 118
    Frank E. Merriweather, Jr. Branch Library, iv, x, 45, 46, 47, 50, 51, 62, 84
    Friendship House and Richard Prosser, 21, 49, 56, 60, 66, 118
Urban Park Housing Development project, 60, 69
urban renewal
    Ellicott District Urban Renewal and Development Authority, xiv, 9
    Frank Reeves Center for Municipal Affairs, 78
    John F. Kennedy Recreation Center, 64
    Urban Park Housing Development, 69
urban transportation, 9–10
    Buffalo Metrorail System, 72
    city and the automobile incompatible, 13
    Lindbergh Center MARTA Station, 30, 32, 73, 117, 118
    Providence Station, 76
    Secretary of Transportation William Coleman, 27, 101

urban unrest, 22, 25
    riots in Los Angeles, Atlanta, and Miami, 41
    riots in Rochester and Watts, 18
Utica Street Subway Station, 32, 61

V
Viner, Gail, AIA, 118
Vosbeck, R. Randall, FAIA, 1, 4, 32, 41, 49, 52, 53, 55, 108, 110, 118, 124

W
Walsh, David, AIA, 118
Washington, Roberta, FAIA, 38–39
waterfronts, 1, 13, 18, 24, 25, 43, 92, 99, 103, 104, 105
    Amistad comes to Buffalo, 43–45
    celebrating the waterfront, 13
    R. B. Fuller links downtown Toronto and its waterfront, 18
    waterfront potential ignored, 24
Wende Correctional Facility, 35, 61
West Seneca Branch Post Office, 60
William-Emslie YMCA, xiv, 34, 61, 71
Wright, Dr. Lydia, 16, 17, 22–23, 24, 60
Wright/Evans weekend house, 16, 17, 60

Y
Yamasaki, Minoru, 5, 95
Young, Whitney M. Jr., 4, 21, 24, 25, 26, 27, 29, 32, 42, 49, 52, 55, 56, 97, 100, 101, 107, 108, 109, 112

Special Thanks

This project could not have been completed without the financial assistance of the many generous individuals who contributed to our Kickstarter fundraising campaign. The success of that project enables us to market and distribute Robert Traynham Coles' memoir, ***Architecture + Advocacy***, to a much wider audience than would have been possible otherwise. We are most grateful to the following for their monetary contributions:

Deborah Abgott
James N. Allen
Meagan Baco
Pat and Dianne Baker
Robert Bates, Architect
Diane L. Bockrath
James A. Brady FAIA
Audre Bunis
Charles H. Campbell
Mary D. and Harold L. Cohen
Dr. Richard K. Dozier
Gerry Evans
Sharon Jordan Holley
Anthony O. James, Architect
Gabriel Kroiz
Jane Liebner
Fern Logan

Ruth Mohn
Michael Puma
Allen Reid
Harry G. Robinson III, FAIA
Dr. Seymour Slavin
Kiernan B Smith
Suzanne Taub
Celestine Traynham-Reid
Cynthia Van Ness
Susan Vasi
Randy Vosbeck, FAIA
Carol B. Wells
Sandy White
Michael V. Wright, AIA
Timothy Sick and Salvatore Zambito

. . . and others who wish to remain anonymous

We especially thank those who contributed at the highest level:

Richard C. Baer
Lauren Belfer
Nancy Belfer
Diana Dillaway
Ken and Monica MacKay
Steve, Heidi and Kieran Meyn

Kathryn Tyler Prigmore, FAIA
Miriam S. Reading
James A. Robinson
Tam and Kevin Rowland
Charles E. Rush, Jr.

On behalf of Robert and Sylvia Coles, and William H. Siener,

Thank you!

Len Kagelmacher
Buffalo Arts Publishing
November 1, 2016

www.ingramcontent.com/pod-product-compliance
Lightning Source LLC
Chambersburg PA
CBHW041127300426
44113CB00003B/88